# TOM NODDY'S

# BUBBLE MAGIC

Running Press • Philadelphia, Pennsylvania

Copyright © 1988 by Tom Noddy.
Printed in the United States of America. All rights reserved under the Pan-American and International Copyright Conventions.

*This book may not be reproduced in whole or in part in any form or by any means, electronic or mechanical, including photocopying, recording, or by any information storage and retrieval system now known or hereafter invented, without written permission from the publisher.*

Canadian representatives: General Publishing Co., Ltd.,
30 Lesmill Road, Don Mills, Ontario M3B 2T6.

International representatives: Worldwide Media Services, Inc.,
115 East Twenty-third Street, New York, NY 10010.

9  8  7  6  5  4  3  2  1

Digit on the right indicates the number of this printing.

Library of Congress Cataloging-in-Publication Number 88-42751

ISBN 0-89471-659-X (paper)
 0-89471-660-3 (library bdg.)
 0-89471-661-1 (package)
Cover design by Toby Schmidt
Interior illustration by Judy Newhouse
Cover and interior photographs by Paul Schraub Photography

This book may be ordered by mail from the publisher.
Please include $1.50 for postage.
*But try your bookstore first!*
Running Press Book Publishers
125 South Twenty-second Street
Philadelphia, Pennsylvania 19103

## ACKNOWLEDGMENTS

I have many people to thank for helping me bring this book together.

Nancy Steele, my patient editor, was able to remember something of her childhood while doing the work of a grownup.

Judy Newhouse amazed me with her illustrations. While reducing bubble forms to two dimensions, she has maintained length, width, and depth–that's magic.

Paul Schraub, a sensitive photographer, had serious fun with this seemingly silly subject.

If there are errors of fact, the fault is mine. Ron Hipschman, a physicist at San Francisco's Exploratorium, did his best to correct some of my more foolish assumptions.

Bob Miller and Frank Oppenheimer of the Exploratorium helped me to see that physics, art, and magic can live happily together in the same sentence.

Eiffel Plasterer has shown me that it is not only possible but a good idea to carry a sense of wonder with you throughout your life.

Carol Fuller deserves credit for providing a room where I could write and a house where I could blow bubbles.

Rory Ostman deserves credit, period.

To Kate O'Bryant,
who knows the best ways
to overcome surface tension

| | |
|---|---|
| Preface: The Bubble Guy . . . . . . . . . . . . . 7 | |
| Introduction . . . . . . . . . . . . . . . . . . . . . . . 10 | |
| ① TOOLS . . . . . . . . . . . . . . . . . . . . . . . . . 12 | |
|    Containers . . . . . . . . . . . . . . . . . . . . . 12 | |
|    Bubble Juice . . . . . . . . . . . . . . . . . . . . 13 | |
|    Wands . . . . . . . . . . . . . . . . . . . . . . . . 14 | |
|    Straws . . . . . . . . . . . . . . . . . . . . . . . . 15 | |
|    Light . . . . . . . . . . . . . . . . . . . . . . . . . 15 | |
| ② BEGINNING BUBBLES . . . . . . . . . . . . . 16 | |
|    Blowing a Bubble . . . . . . . . . . . . . . . . 17 | |
|    Aim . . . . . . . . . . . . . . . . . . . . . . . . . . 21 | |
|    Pop! What Breaks Bubbles? . . . . . . . . . 22 | |
|    Bouncing a Bubble . . . . . . . . . . . . . . . 24 | |
|    Two Wands . . . . . . . . . . . . . . . . . . . . 28 | |
|    The Inside-Out Bubble . . . . . . . . . . . . . 31 | |
|    Bubbles Inside Bubbles . . . . . . . . . . . . 35 | |
|    Good Clean Fun . . . . . . . . . . . . . . . . . 38 | |
|       Homemade Juice . . . . . . . . . . . . . 38 | |
|       Bathtub Bubbles . . . . . . . . . . . . . 39 | |
|       Whale-sized Bubbles . . . . . . . . . . . 39 | |
| ③ BEYOND ROUND BUBBLES . . . . . . . . 41 | |
|    Wiggly Worms . . . . . . . . . . . . . . . . . . 42 | |

The Bubble Cube . . . . . . . . . . . . . . . . . 45
The Carousel . . . . . . . . . . . . . . . . . . . . 53
The Jewel . . . . . . . . . . . . . . . . . . . . . . 58
④ COSMIC BUBBLES . . . . . . . . . . . . . . . . 64
   Galactica . . . . . . . . . . . . . . . . . . . . . . 65
   The Caterpillar . . . . . . . . . . . . . . . . . . 68
   The Love Bubble . . . . . . . . . . . . . . . . 72
⑤ FIZZIX . . . . . . . . . . . . . . . . . . . . . . . . . 76
   Water . . . . . . . . . . . . . . . . . . . . . . . . 77
   Soap . . . . . . . . . . . . . . . . . . . . . . . . . 77
   Pressure . . . . . . . . . . . . . . . . . . . . . . 79
   Angles . . . . . . . . . . . . . . . . . . . . . . . 79
   Suds . . . . . . . . . . . . . . . . . . . . . . . . . 80
   Colors . . . . . . . . . . . . . . . . . . . . . . . . 81
⑥ A MAGIC NATION . . . . . . . . . . . . . . . . 85
   Eiffel . . . . . . . . . . . . . . . . . . . . . . . . . 86
   The Bubble Brat . . . . . . . . . . . . . . . . . 89
   Mustache . . . . . . . . . . . . . . . . . . . . . 90
   Busking in Berkeley . . . . . . . . . . . . . . . 91
   Rick's Story . . . . . . . . . . . . . . . . . . . . 93
   Obsession . . . . . . . . . . . . . . . . . . . . . 94
Bubbliography . . . . . . . . . . . . . . . . . . . . 95

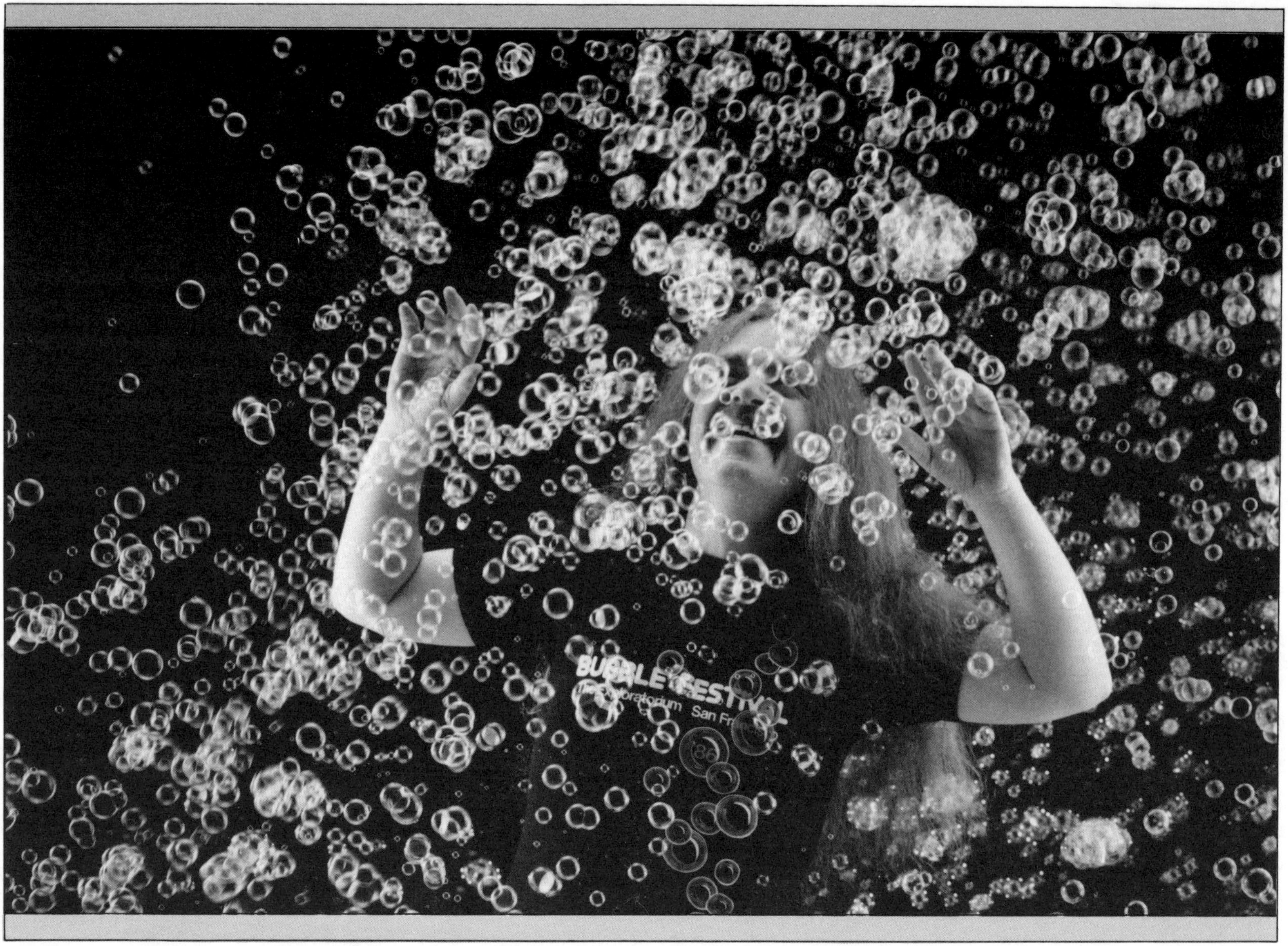

# PREFACE: THE BUBBLE GUY

As a kid, I was a daydreamer. I got pretty good grades in school, but I spent more class time walking on the ceiling and flying over the playground than doing my schoolwork. I'd come in for a landing long enough to answer the teachers' questions, but most of my questions were answered in daydreams.

I remember trying to figure out grownups. They knew a lot, but if they all were kids once, they must have forgotten a lot. Every kid that I ever met was able to transform ordinary sticks into magical wands, breathe life into lifeless objects, talk to animals, and fly as far as we could imagine —and we could all imagine very far.

The grownups would sometimes talk about these things, and they had names for some of them. I liked it when I heard a grownup say that something was "in my imagination." It sounded like a place you could go, "a magic nation." But the grownups seemed to have forgotten how to use the magic wands, and there were some things they just couldn't see. Even when they tried to play, they couldn't stay with it for hours the way we did. It takes a long time to explore a nation as big as this one.

It worried me when they said that I would grow up. I wanted to be bigger and I wanted to be able to drive a car, and stay up late, and do other grownup things, but I didn't want to forget the things that kids know. When I was seven years old, I went to a magic place in a dark room, closed my eyes, crossed my fingers, scrunched my toes, and promised that I wouldn't forget. I repeated the promise over and over to make it stronger.

I grew up near New York City, in an industrial city called Paterson, New Jersey. I wasn't one of the toughest guys in school, but some of my friends were. I remember that at some point even the other kids started telling each other to "grow up" and "quit acting like a kid." I tried.

I went to college in Memphis, Tennessee, in 1967, an exciting time. A lot of us kids thought that we could change the real world with magic. One of my best friends in Memphis was a girl named Rory. Rory was my age, and she had a quick mind and a sharp tongue, but she also had toys. Rory was good with a yo-yo, great at jacks, and she was the best bubble-blower I had ever seen: she blew grapefruit-sized bubbles.

I learned a lot from Rory; while she was growing up without forgetting, she even helped me remember the day when I went to that dark room and crossed my fingers and promised not to forget.

Many years after I had stopped playing with toys, I found that I could work them better. Back in elementary school, I could get a yo-yo to do a "loop-de-loop," but I couldn't "rock the cradle." As a grownup, I was a bit more coordinated and I could stay in the real world long enough to learn the moves. By the time I was in college, I could figure out, practice, and accomplish tricks with yo-yos, spinning tops, magnets, and bubbles as well as the tricks with typewriters, mathematics, and English composition that my teachers were teaching. In those years, I learned that I didn't have to choose between learning to be a grownup and "acting like a kid"; sometimes I'd stay up late *and* play with bubbles.

In 1969 and '70, I hitchhiked up the East Coast to Canada, down to the Gulf of Mexico, out to the West Coast, and then back East. I had no money, but I told good stories and people helped me along. I started writing puppet plays, and when I saw Rory again, this time in New York, she gave me some hand puppets that she had made. I started performing on the streets as Tom Noddy and the Travelin' Puppets–political, social, and spiritual satire with hand puppets.

When I finally went home to New Jersey–to live with my parents and take a job–it was for the purpose of saving money to fly to Europe. As soon as I took the job, I set a mental deadline for quitting. I decided to work for ten months, save all the money that I could, and then take the money to Europe. I didn't want to spend my money by going out at night, so I bought a jar of dime-store bubble juice to entertain myself at home. I worked every weekday, and weekends if I could. Almost every night, I'd sit at home blowing bubbles. Almost every night, for ten months.

On some weekends, I'd go to Central Park in New York City and use a few bubble tricks that I'd taught myself to attract the attention of a small crowd for my puppet show. Then I began performing indoors at a poet's café in Paterson. The bubbles were much better inside, out of the wind, and my bubble show really started there, in a café called The Bottom of the Barrel.

Becoming known as the Bubble Guy has meant that I've become a magnet for bubble information. If people know anything about bubbles, they tell me. Sometimes it's something about the physics of bubbles, or it may be an interesting experience someone has had with bubbles. Once in a while, in the early days, I'd meet someone who'd show me a bubble trick; a stranger in Oregon first showed me the Bubble Inside a Bubble. Some people whom I've taught have taught me; David the Minstrel showed me the Carousel, and a musician named Bill helped me find the Bubble Cube.

Bubbles aren't much, really–just a little liquid soap and a breath of air. But they have opened my mind to science while keeping me in the company of kids, and they help me stay in touch with that magic nation that meant so much when I was seven years old. It's a good idea to remember what we knew as kids; who knows, life might be a cumulative test. Fortunately, there are plenty of seven-year-old teachers.

# INTRODUCTION

Blow a bubble.
    Catch it on the wand.
    Hold it in the light.
    Watch it till it pops.
    Blow a bigger bubble, catch it, hold it, watch it. Blow another bubble…
    If you do a little of that, you'll be rewarded with simple beauty. If you do that a lot, you'll develop a new skill and a reputation as an eccentric.
    It's unlikely that this new skill will bring you any financial reward, but an ability to bring beauty into your life will serve you well anywhere in the world.
    As for your reputation, you can defend yourself by citing the names of other noted bubble enthusiasts: Sir Isaac

Newton, the 18th-century mathematician who brought science into the modern age; Joseph Plateau, the blind Belgian physicist whose experiments with soap bubbles in the 19th century provided answers and questions for some of the brightest scientific minds of our era; and C.V. Boys, the brilliant British experimentalist whose turn-of-the-century book on the subject is still published, studied, and taught in our universities. Even today, numerous physicists, mathematicians, chemists, biologists, architects, and astronomers turn to soap bubbles as models to help us understand the way our universe works. So you could claim that your interest in bubbles is dispassionate, intellectual curiosity. But don't think that you'll be able to fool me.

I know that if you spend any time gazing at those liquid spheres, you'll see some of what I've seen. The perfection of form can be described as "the electromagnetic effects of surface tension and compressional energy," but it has another effect that is infinitely more difficult to describe. The flow of iridescent colors may well be wave interference patterns, but they are also stunningly beautiful. Mathematics may be able to explain why a froth of multifaceted bubbles fit together to form a perfectly balanced, three-dimensional network, but science doesn't even attempt to explain why that is so pleasing to us. When wondering at the simple beauty of a soap bubble we may turn to science to seek answers, but our sense of wonder stimulates something more than just questions.

# TOOLS................You'll need only a few common, inexpensive items to produce any of the bubble forms described in this book.

## Containers

I was once told by a man in the bubble business that the original commercial bubble liquid was sold by pharmacists in the same four-ounce glass jars that were used to dispense liquid medicines. That, he suggested, is the reason for the shape of today's bubble jars. Whether this is true or not, the shape of the American bubble container has been the same since I was a little bubble-blowing boy. Now most bubble juice is sold in plastic jars of various sizes, but these jars are still the same basic shape.

These little containers are very convenient for holding

in your hand while dipping the wand. Unfortunately, this little convenience has also been largely responsible for banishing bubbles from the friendly, windless living rooms of our houses. My advice is this: before you blow the first bubble, *pour the juice into another container.*

You know what usually happens when you hand a jar of bubbles to a kid: her eyes light up as she unscrews the cap and takes out the wand. Then she blows a stream of bubbles into the air. In that triumphant moment, she stretches out one hand to catch a bubble, and in the same instant her face drops as she realizes, too late, that her other hand has spilled the juice onto her shoe. At that sad and humiliating moment, we sometimes react without thinking. We exclaim, "I knew it! How many times have I told you to watch what you're doing? If you can't pay attention…" After a few experiences like that, only Grandma buys the bubbles.

Hold on! What are we really saying when we hand over that bottle of liquid? "Here, this gets wet and slippery. Hold it in your hand and run after the bubbles, but don't spill it–I'll get mad."

What are we thinking when we say, "Watch what you're doing"? She has created liquid spheres, transparent and reflective, glowing with iridescent colors, floating on the gentlest breeze, and we want her to watch what? That plastic jar?

Pour the juice into a bowl, a big bowl that no one would even think of holding in their hands (maybe some plastic kitchen bowl or a doggie bowl with a wide bottom; they're designed not to spill). With a bowl of juice sitting on the ground or on a table, the whole game becomes "dip and blow." Then the bubble blower has both hands free, you don't have to worry about a big mess, it's easier to share the juice, and the game doesn't end with someone sad and someone mad.

## Bubble Juice

Watching me perform, people often suppose that I'm using a special bubble solution–they think that I've added glycerin or sugar or something. If I did make a stronger solution, most of the bubbles that I create in my show wouldn't work.

You can make all of the bubbles described in this book using the commercial bubble juice sold in dime stores. That's what I use. Some brands are better than others, but I know of three widely available brands that I could use for my show: Wonder Bubbles, Pustifix and Bubble-Os. If you have some other mixture, you'll be able to do some forms, but probably not all.

Different kinds of bubble juice act differently. My friend Eiffel G. Plasterer, who mixes his own bubble solutions, uses nine formulas which he describes as being either "fast" or "slow" and which produce bubbles that are "wet" or "dry," "heavy" or "light." His curiosity and intelligence have led him to solve individual bubble problems with individual "solutions."

Dishwashing liquid mixed with water will make beautiful bubbles. In fact, this "fast" solution can produce some of the biggest bubbles you've ever seen, but it would be very difficult to keep these fast bubbles alive long enough to build a Bubble Jewel. If you make a mixture that produces "strong" (long-lasting) bubbles, you'll probably find that it is also "slow," and a slow-moving film isn't good for some tricks, such as the Bubbles Inside Bubbles described on page 35.

The strongest soap bubble solution that I've ever seen is Eiffel Plasterer's private "Long-lived Bubbline" formula. The bubbles are thick and their liquid drains very slowly. Eiffel keeps them around for months, but when I dipped a wand into the mixture and blew, it wouldn't even "bub!" Eiffel uses a specially designed device to slow down his breath so that it gently inflates that "strong" bubble.

Some of the literature in the Bubbliography, page 95, will tell you how to make strong, long-lasting bubbles. If you want to try fast, big bubbles, turn to "Good Clean Fun," page 38.

If the juice is extremely cold, it will be slower. If it gets too hot, it will be faster, and you may need to add a little water after a while to compensate for evaporation. Don't worry if you see dirt, sticks, or little bugs in the juice; as long as these things are wet, they won't affect the bubbles.

## Wands

When I was a kid, bubble juice and plastic wands were sold together in glass jars, and the plastic wands had identical little circles on each end. By the time I rediscovered bubbles, the jars were plastic but the wands were still the same. To get enough juice for a melon-sized bubble, I developed a "triple dip" method (my first bubble trick). After a while some brilliant toy designer invented wands with little ridges around one of the circles. The ridges hold more juice; this means bigger bubbles and more bubbles on a single blow. (Sometimes the gradual evolution of humankind is marked by a quantum leap.)

If you find yourself without a ridged wand (the thick ones with deep ridges are the best), you can make a wand that's just as good by using ordinary cotton pipe cleaners (not the "special" multicolored ones; those are usually made of a material that doesn't stay wet). Just bend one end around into a loop and twist it closed. The fuzzy cotton holds extra juice just like the ridges on the plastic wands. The cotton that is on the stem of this wand holds juice, too–extra juice that will drip onto the bubble, add too much weight, and make a mess. If possible, the cotton should be burned off the handle (by an adult) so that you have a wand with a wire handle and a fuzzy loop. You can add more length and stability by attaching more wire; better still, use the wire to attach the loop to a stick (or pencil, or straw).

Once you have a good wand, save it and keep extras around. If you're blowing bubbles from a bowl, several people can dip in at the same time. Six wands, no waiting!

## Straws

By using a straw, you can more easily control where your bubbles go, and how big they'll be. Someone once gave me a silver straw, and except for the extra weight, it works just as well as plastic. You can use any straw as long as it's made of a material that will stay wet, but I just use cheap plastic straws like the ones that you get free when you buy a soft drink. Paper straws will work, but not for long. Wide straws hold bubbles better.

Since you can see the end of a straw, you can see where your bubbles will emerge. Just dip the straw into the juice and place the wet end where you want a bubble to be–attached to another bubble, inside a bubble, or even within a cluster of bubbles–and gently blow.

A straw is especially useful when you want to control the size of a bubble. When it's blown through a straw, a bubble grows more gradually. If you make the bubble too large, you can suck out some of the air before withdrawing the straw. There are other tricks for increasing the size of a finished bubble or eliminating accidental bubbles (see page 34).

## Light

If you blow bubbles on a sunny day, you'll see the sun reflected twice on each bubble. If you turn your back to the sun, the reflections will appear once on the convex surface nearest you, and again (but upside down!) on the concave wall inside at the back of the bubble. If you blow bubbles on a bright cloudy day, you'll see the whole sky reflected twice, and if you look closely, you'll see the whole horizon.

Whatever is brightest in your environment will show up best on the bubble; outside on a dark night, you'll see the reflections of streetlights, windows of houses, the campfire, or the moon. Inside you might see a lampshade or the entire room. You'll notice that one reflection is right side up and the other upside down!

Colors on bubbles show up best in brightly lit areas. Sunny days are nice; the two little suns gleam in each bubble. But when nearly the whole bubble is lit by a bright cloudy sky, you'll have the best view of the gorgeous iridescent colors, especially if you view it with a shaded building, a black cloth, a tree, or another dark surface as its backdrop. Under these ideal conditions, you'll be able to look into something so thin that it's almost not there. Surprising how real it is.

# BEGINNING BUBBLES........

This chapter contains a step-by-step (blow-by-blow) account of how to blow a bubble, bounce a bubble, and blow bubbles inside bubbles. As you learn these basic forms you'll be learning how to avoid popping bubbles and how to hold the weight of a bubble. These are the basic skills necessary for all Bubble Magic. Once you can do these, I think you'll be amazed at how quickly you learn to build more complex forms.

If you have trouble making one of the bubbles in this chapter, go on to the next one.

After the directions for each bubble you'll find suggestions on how to solve any problems you may have.

# BLOWING A BUBBLE

Almost everyone has done it, but blowing a single bubble and holding it on the wand is a knack that your hands may not always remember. Your mind can help.

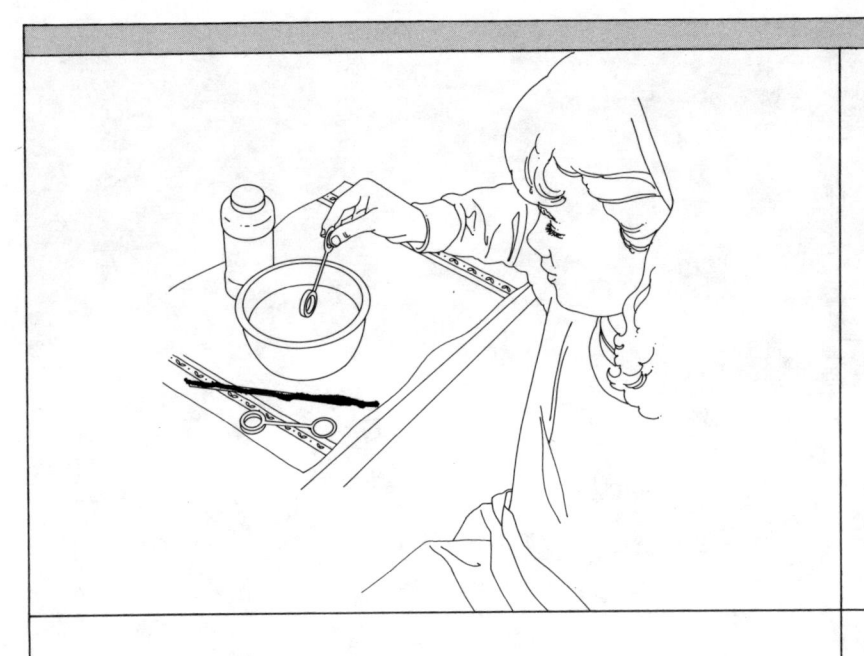

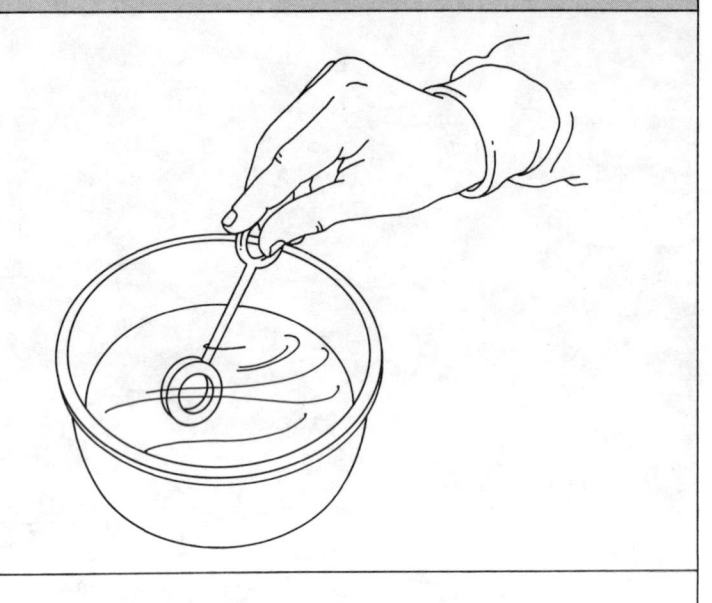

**1. Get set.**

You'll need bubble juice, a bowl to hold the liquid, two wands, a drinking straw, and a windless place. If you are indoors, you'll want to have a towel or other cloth to catch the drips.

Pour the juice into the bowl.

**2. Dip the wand.**

Hold the wand at the very end, opposite the blowing end. You don't need to swish the wand up and down; that just makes suds. Dip it into the liquid deep enough to submerge the hole and wet some of the stem, and take it out.

**3. Hold the wand in front of your mouth.**
   Your hand should be a couple of inches in front of your cheek, a bit below your eye, with the wand horizontal.

**4. Pucker up.**
   Pucker your lips into a little round whistling shape.

**5. Blow.**
   Aim at the sheet of film and blow a stream of air. If you miss, nothing will happen (except that you may laugh; and if you're lucky, you might accidentally laugh out a stream of small bubbles).

*Beginning Bubbles*

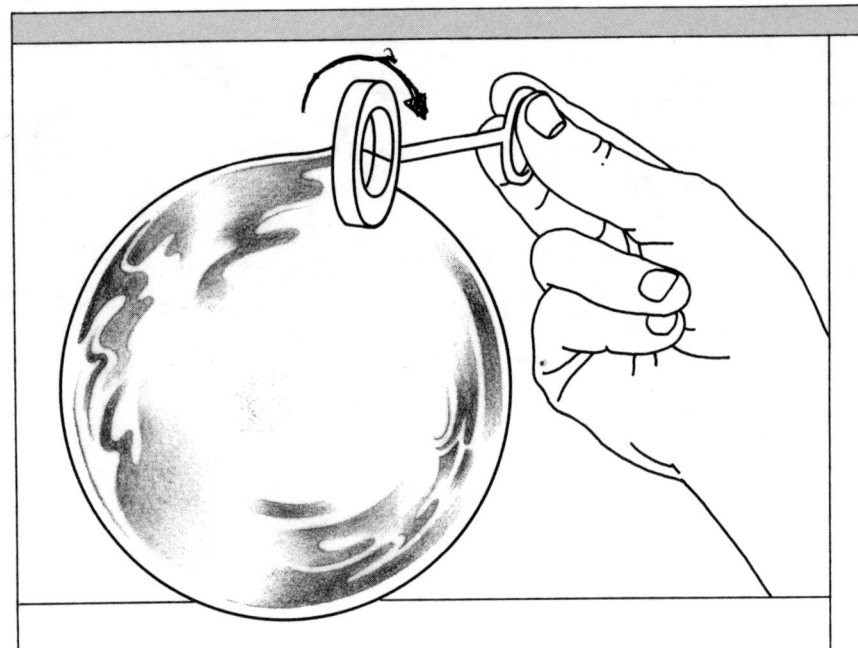

6. Flip the wand over to close the hole you've been blowing through.

If you don't close the hole, the air will rush back out and the bubble will deflate. You could close the hole by letting the bubble go and then catching it gently from above, but if you flip the wand, you won't need to catch the bubble.

When the bubble is as big as you want it to be, stop blowing and rotate your wrist toward you so that the ring of the wand flips over to close the hole. The bubble will slide down and hang from the wand. Because you haven't lost contact with the bubble, you don't have to worry about catching it—you're still holding it.

# PROBLEMS?

At this point, there are only a few things that can go wrong. Assuming that you're not trying to do this in the midst of a dust storm or child-care center, the problem is easy to solve. For example:

*You blow, but nothing happens.*

If the film broke, you blew too hard or waited too long before blowing. Try holding the wand a little farther away from your mouth. If the film is still there after you blow, you could have blown too softly, but more likely, your aim was off. (See "Aim," page 21.)

*You blow, and a stream of little bubbles flies **straight off the wand**.*

You blew a bit too hard. Blow a little more softly or move the wand away from your mouth a bit more.

*You blow, and little bubbles fly off in a fast stream at an angle from the wand.*

Your aim is off. Some of the air is hitting the film but it's hitting at an angle, causing the bubbles to close off as they slide over the edge of the wand. (See "Aim," page 21.)

*You're able to get a bubble, but it jiggles, shakes, distorts, and then deflates. It won't grow.*

Your aim might have started OK, but then the air started to divide on the wand: some went in, maintaining the bubble, but some was split off by the wand and struck the

Tom Noddy's Bubble Magic

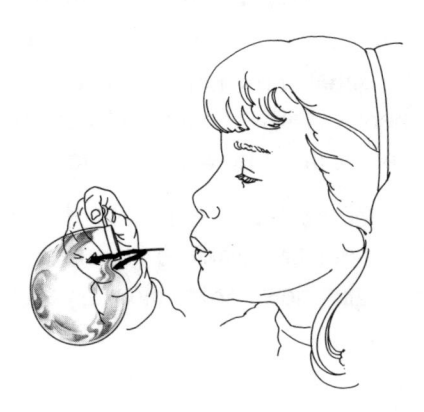

outside of the bubble, disturbing it. (See "Aim.")

●*You blow a bubble, but it pops before it gets very big.*

It probably touched something dry: your hand? a dry part of the wand? your hair? your shirt cuff?

Dip the wand again, deep into the container. Hold your hand up with your fingers curled against your palm. (Check the drawing on page 19 to see how to hold the wand.) If you're still having trouble, see page 22, "POP! What Breaks Bubbles?"

●*You blow a big bubble, but then it falls off the wand.*

You're doing great! You blew a bubble large enough to fall from its own weight. Now turn to page 28 to see how you can use two wands to hold up a big bubble.

If the bubbles are mysteriously breaking, see page 22 for "POP!"

## AIM

*If you're having trouble with your aim, try this:*

Hold your hand a couple of inches in front of your face and blow at it. You can feel where your breath is hitting. Is it straight ahead? If not, change your lip arrangement until it is. Now use that same lip arrangement for bubble blowing.

*Or try this:*

Through puckered lips, blow as straight as possible into the wand. Now, *while holding your head still,* slowly move the wand around in front of your mouth. When your aim is close you'll see the film stretch and start a bubble that jiggles around. When your aim is right you'll see the bubble growing without jiggling. That's the spot! Check out that position–that's where you want to hold the wand for your blow.

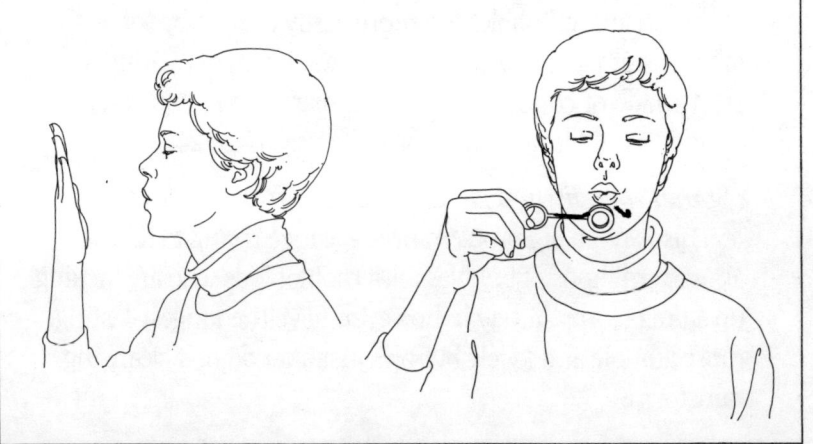

*Beginning Bubbles*

# POP!
# WHAT BREAKS BUBBLES?

You can create longer-lasting bubbles if you understand some of the things that cause them to burst.

Hold the wand at the end, as far away from the bubble as possible. Pull your hair back. Keep the wand one or two inches away from your mouth. If your hand is underneath the bubble as you're blowing, that growing bubble is doomed as soon as it gets big enough, so hold the bubble from above, with your hand up by your cheekbone. You'll have better control there anyway.

Here are some things to watch out for:

- *Something dry*–a dry wand, a dry straw, a dry fly, or almost anything dry.

Keep the wands and straw wet. They needn't be drippy, just wet. If they're out in the air too long, they'll dry out.

Surprisingly, bubbles are more easily broken by some fabrics, such as polyester, than others. If you're wearing a shirt made of cotton, wool, linen, or raw silk, you can bounce a bubble on your shirtsleeve; see page 24.

- *Something dirty*–dust, dirt, salt, or other air pollutants.

This is not a big problem unless you're trying to fill the air with millions of bubbles for a mob of kids who are kicking up a dust storm. You will, however, have the longest-lasting, most durable and lovely bubbles just after a good cleansing rainstorm.

In fact, if you find yourself outside during a gentle rain, you'll see that raindrops don't break bubbles; they either hit the bubbles, slide down, and drip off, or they drive right through the bubbles without popping them. In a real downpour, of course, the drops hit too hard and break the bubbles.

- *Very rough treatment*–blowing too hard, from too close.

Bubbles are incredibly flexible, but there is a limit. If you have trouble judging how hard to blow, try moving the wand a bit farther away.

- *Evaporation.*

On a hot, dry sunny day or in a dry, heated room, the water in a bubble is more quickly drawn out into the air, and the bubble will dry up and pop. When the juice gets hot, the bubbles are thinner, the juice drains faster, and so the bubbles pop sooner. On a very hot day, it helps to chill the juice in the fridge or a cooler.

The opposite is also true. During or after a good soaking rain, bubbles last longer and will rest on wet grass, bushes, trees, or mud.

- *Gravity.*

Bubbles seem to defy the laws of gravity. The effects of surface tension and air movement are so much more pronounced than gravity that in many experiments conducted by scientists, gravity's effect is regarded as negligible. But eventually, this all-pervasive force will have its way.

The liquid that forms the bubble swirls around as you blow it, then begins to settle toward the bottom as the top gets thinner and thinner. If something else doesn't pop the bubble first, you can watch the top become colorless and actually invisible! Finally, when the top of the bubble is too thin to support its own weight, it pops.

### ◦ *Kids!*

Kids (of all ages) can't resist popping bubbles; maybe that's because a bubble is one of the only things in the world they're allowed to break. Kids have some cause to believe that this is their inalienable right. They may not be able to explain to you exactly why that is; it seems self-evident. Keep this in mind when negotiating a fair agreement.

*Beginning Bubbles*

# BOUNCING A BUBBLE

People who have watched me bounce a bubble on my arm like a tennis ball insist that I'm using some exotic bubble concoction. They're sure that every bubble that they've ever blown has burst as soon as it touched anything. You've seen bubbles pop when they hit your finger or a wood floor, but you also may have seen them bounce on a rug and rest for a bit before disappearing.

Some fabrics do not readily break bubbles. Cotton is good; linen is OK; wool is great! Polyester and the kind of nylon that's used to make baseball jackets and windbreakers pop bubbles quickly, and so does leather. My guess is that the differences are related to the kinds of oil in the fabric—cottonseed oil, lanolin, or petroleum—and the static electrical charge.

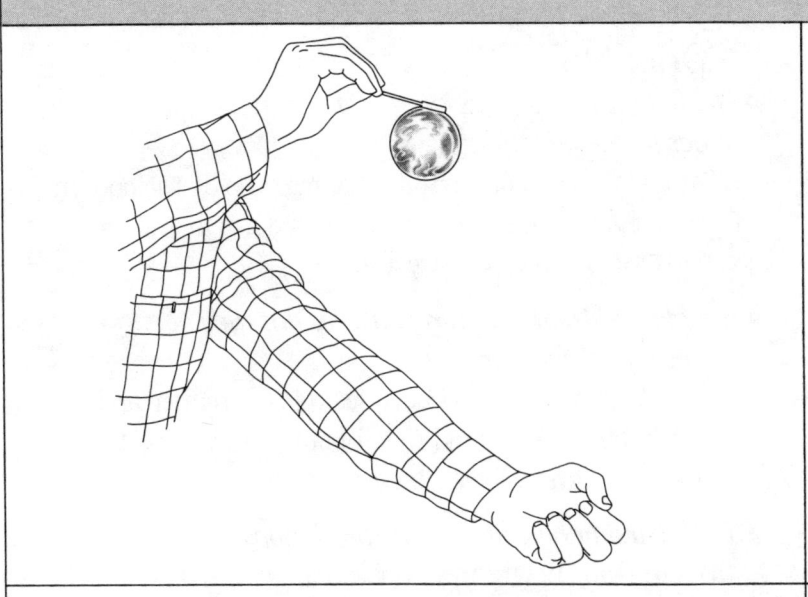

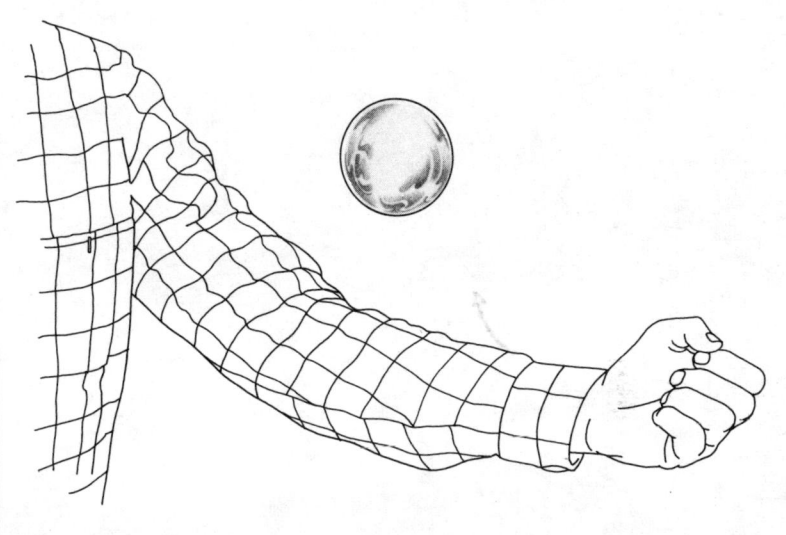

My friend, Kate, used silk to make a shirt for me to wear when I perform. I was worried because I'd seen bubbles pop on silk. But she used raw silk, which has a lot of natural oil, and it bounced bubbles as well as wool. Many silk shirts are made of sheer silk, but to make sheer silk, raw silk must be "cooked" (to remove some oil) and treated with salt, and salt is never good for bubbles. The result is that raw silk bounces bubbles, but sheer silk pops them.

Try this while wearing a long-sleeved cotton shirt or wool sweater:

1. Blow a lemon-sized bubble and hold your arm straight out.

2. Toss the bubble up.

*Beginning Bubbles*

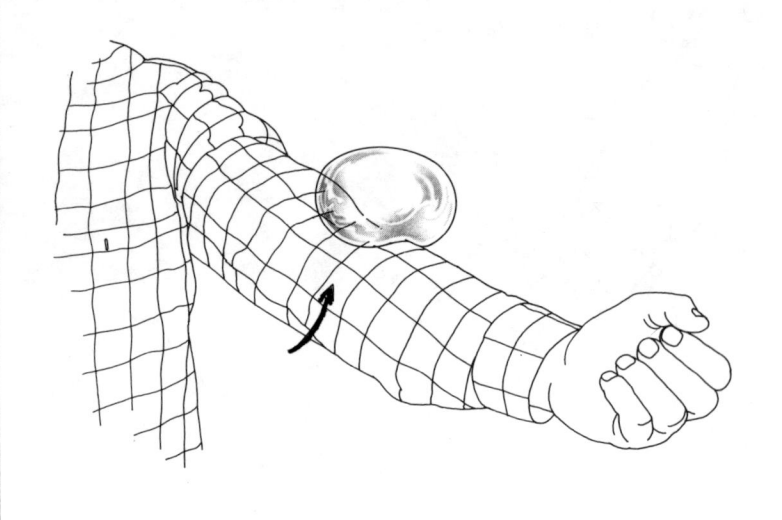

**3. Give it a light bop.**
You can bounce it to the other arm, to your knee, to a friend, or to anything made of "bubble-friendly" material. If it falls too low for you to get under it, remember that you can always catch it on the wand again, lift it up and toss it again.

# PROBLEMS?

• *The bubble falls so quickly that you can't get your arm under it soon enough.*

The bubble could be too wet. That big drop on the bottom causes it to fall much faster. You can wait for it to drip, or learn to drain it a bit (see page 44).

• *You blow a stream of many bubbles but they pop, even on your wool sweater.*

Several bubbles blown at once seem to be thinner, and thinner bubbles can't stand much bouncing. The best bouncer is the first bubble after a fresh dip.

• *It's the first bubble after a dip, but it pops anyway.*

It's surprising how sturdy bubbles can be, but it is possible to hit them *too* hard.

The problem could be your shirt; patches of dirt will break bubbles even if the fabric won't. Remember to watch out for buttons, snaps, and your own skin.

• *It worked for a while, but then the bubbles started to pop.*

Once part of the fabric gets wet from bursting a bubble or from absorbing a drop of juice, that spot isn't so good any more. Twist your sleeve around or just try another spot.

A little boy who was trying to learn how to bounce bubbles once taught me another trick. He was too excited to be gentle enough to bounce a bubble, but he was wearing a good bubble-bouncing shirt. I tossed a bubble over to him and he swung his thin little arm at it much too quickly. But instead of breaking it, his arm went right through and split it into two bubbles. I've since learned to do this by moving my arm quickly, but it usually only works at the thinnest part of my wrist, and only in good weather. Part of the problem is that my arms are too big. This is one trick that little kids can do more easily than grownups.

*Beginning Bubbles*

# TWO WANDS

With two wands, you can hold up a much bigger bubble. When I first started blowing bubbles, I tried to make them bigger and bigger. I found that after a bubble reached a certain size, it would fall off the wand, just as a gathering drop of water falls from a faucet after it gains enough weight.

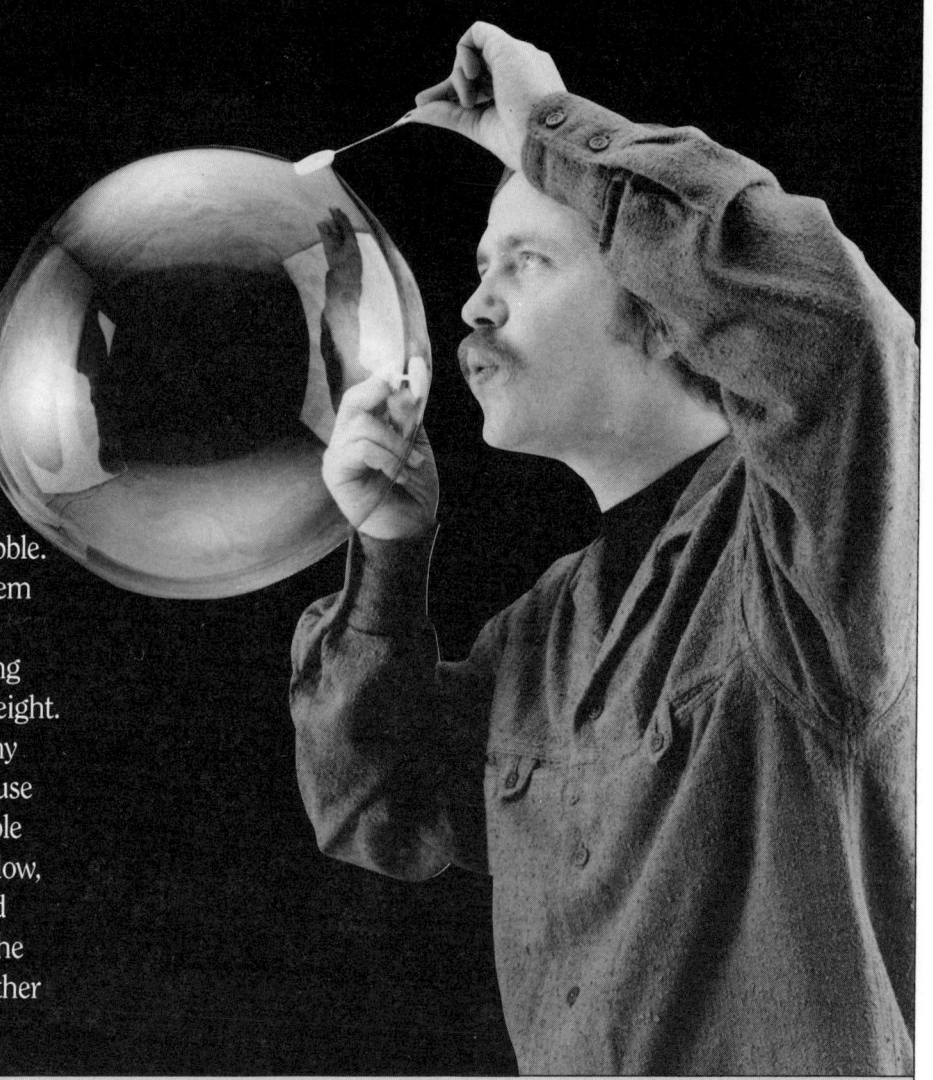

For a while I worked at holding the bubble up with my breath while I was blowing. This was pretty tricky, because I soon had to take another breath. When I did, the bubble started to fall and I had to come back in with my next blow, quickly but not hard. If I wasn't quick, the bubble would deflate, and if I blew too hard, the bubble would fly off the wand. It's a strange breathing technique useful for no other purpose that I can think of, but I became good at it (a truly inane skill). It took the longest time to figure out that all I had to do was *hold* the bubble up with another wand.

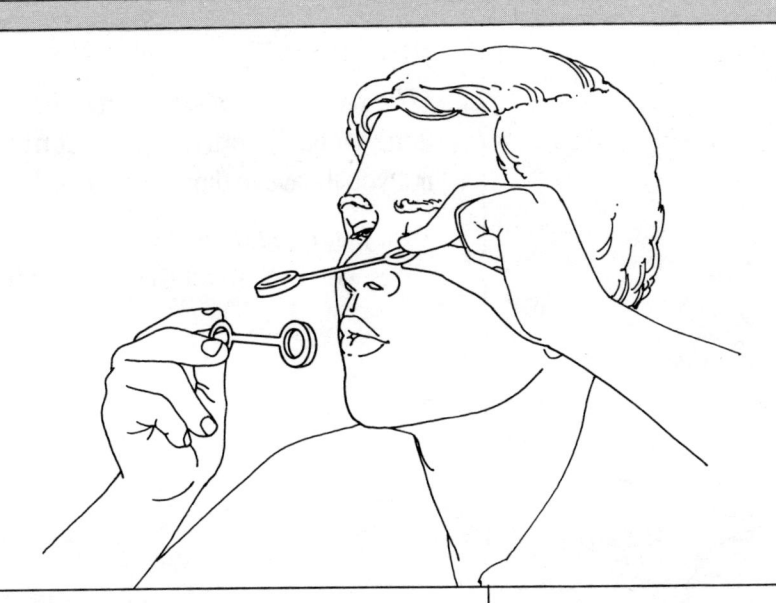

This was a real breakthrough! With the wand in my left hand holding up a bubble, the other wand was free to leave the bubble, get more juice, and get into position for adding more bubbles. The wand in my right hand became very active; but the only job for my left-hand wand was to help hold up the bubbles. When the bubbles got heavy, I could hold them up with both wands.

The second wand doesn't need to be drippy, but it must be wet; if it dries out it will pop the bubble.

Using two wands takes a little getting used to, but then it makes everything easier. After figuring out how to use two wands, I was soon able to create Bubble Magic–and so can you. Here's how to begin:

1. Hold the first wand in front of your mouth, with the second wand perched above, ready to touch and hold the emerging bubble.

*Beginning Bubbles*

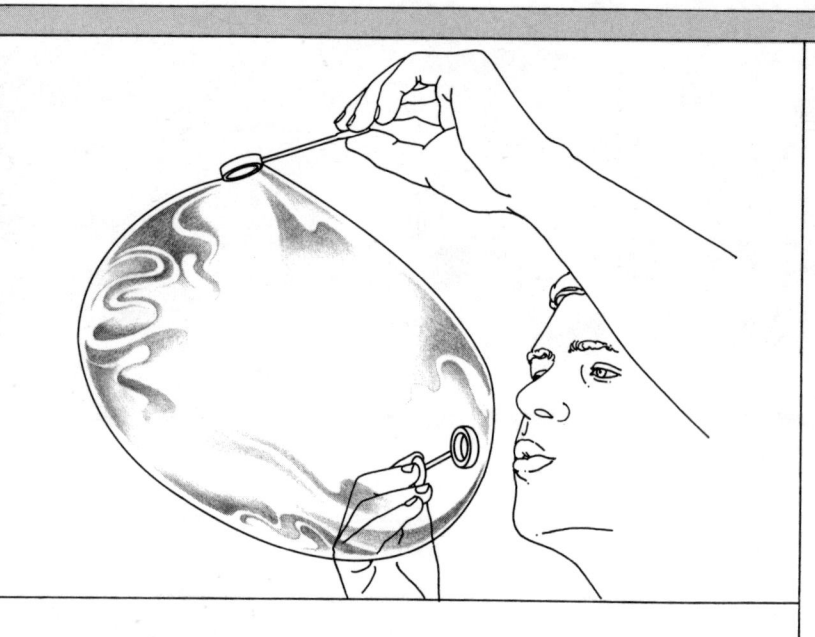

2. Keeping the left wand flat on top of the bubble, you can now steer this fluid form up away from your chin or just hold it in place.

## PROBLEMS?
*The second wand keeps breaking the bubble.*
  It's probably gotten dry. You don't have to dip it often, but you'll have to dip now and again to keep it wet.

*You just can't do it.*
  Yes, you can, and it makes everything easier.

# THE INSIDE-OUT BUBBLE

The inside-out bubble is a cheap trick. It's good for a cheap laugh, but sometimes that is all you can afford. Sometimes that's all you need!

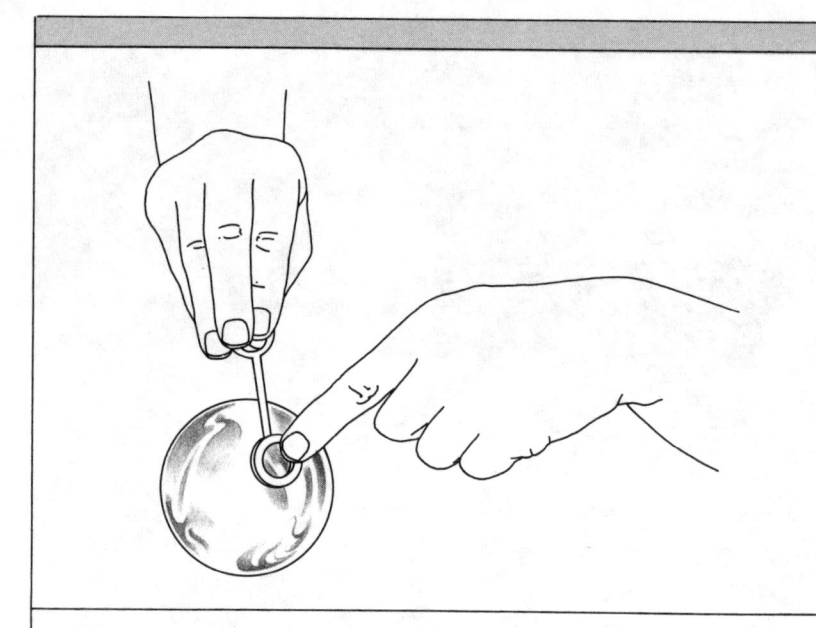

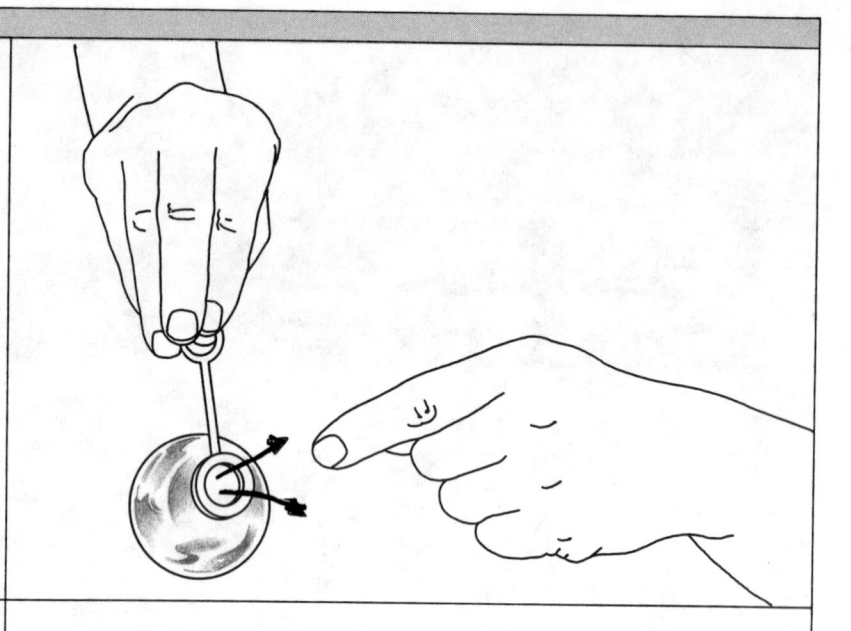

1. Blow a bubble and hold it on the wand. With a dry finger, touch the sheet of film that is stretched across the hole of the wand.

2. Take your finger away and watch the bubble deflate back up to the wand.

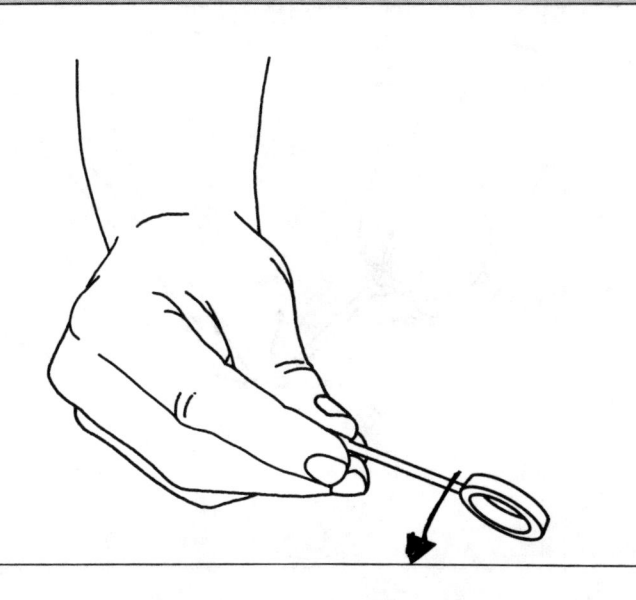

3. After the bubble deflates, turn the wand over and blow again. Show the new bubble and say, "Now it's inside-out." (Wait for the delayed response from your audience, and be prepared to hear a groan.)

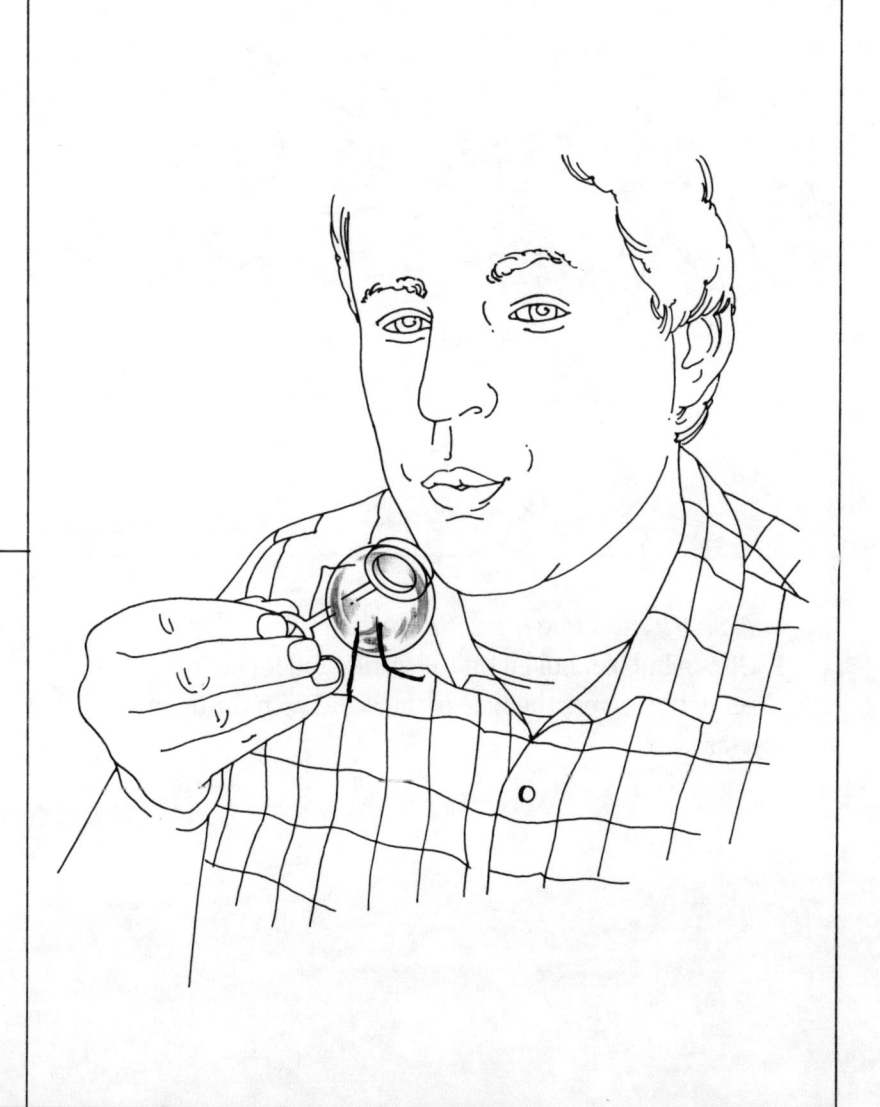

*Beginning Bubbles*

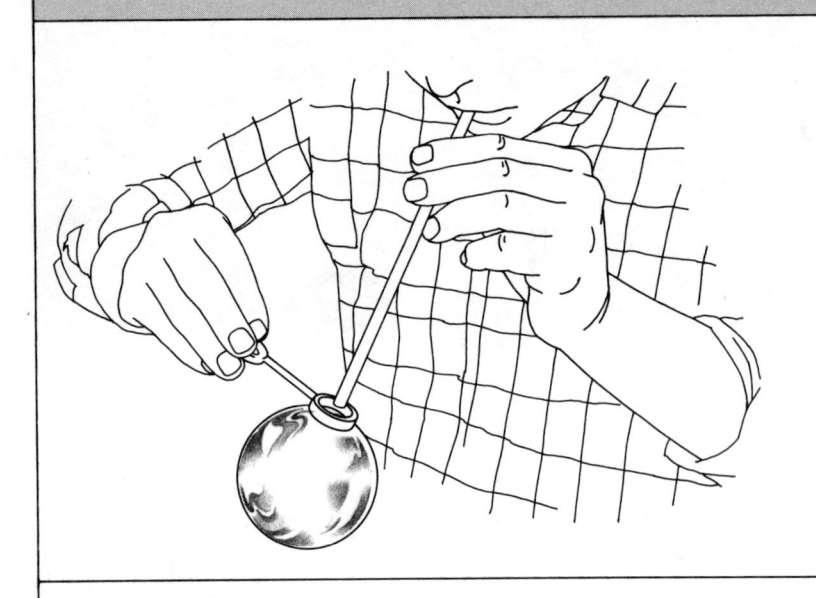

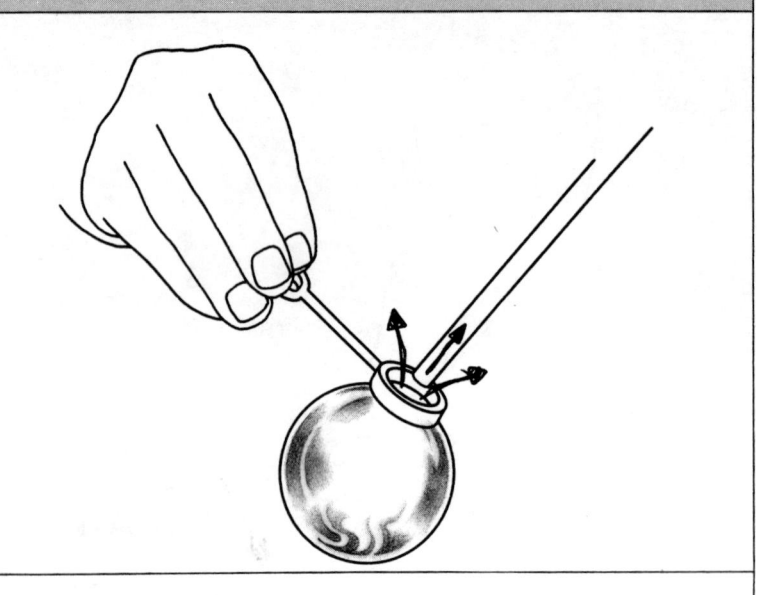

*Now try the same thing this way:*
1. Blow a bubble, hold it on the wand, and touch the sheet of film across the hole of the wand with the tip of a wet straw.

2. Now suck just a little air through the straw. If the end of the straw is actually touching the film, that film across the hole will break and the bubble will deflate.

This little trick with the straw will work for any sheet of soap film. If you touch the straw to a wall dividing two bubbles and suck, you'll eliminate that wall and make one bubble out of two. This will help you correct mistakes! You can eliminate accidental little bubbles and go on to accomplish bubble tricks that aren't as cheap as this one.

# BUBBLES INSIDE BUBBLES

If you look at the hole in a wand after you've dipped it into the juice, you'll see a sheet of soap film—and if you blow at it, you can make a bubble.

If you look at a bubble after you've blown it, you'll see that the same film is now a sphere—and if you blow at it, you can make another bubble. This new bubble will be trapped inside the first bubble.

Making the second bubble is a little trickier, because this time the soap film has a curved surface and it isn't being held as steadily as the one in the wand, but the principle is the same. The idea is to blow a big bubble, hold it steady, and direct a short burst of air toward it.

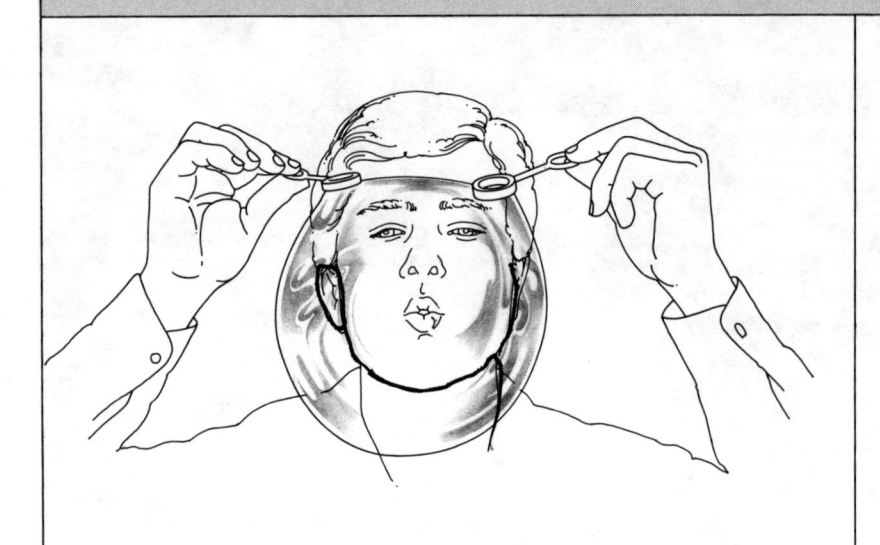

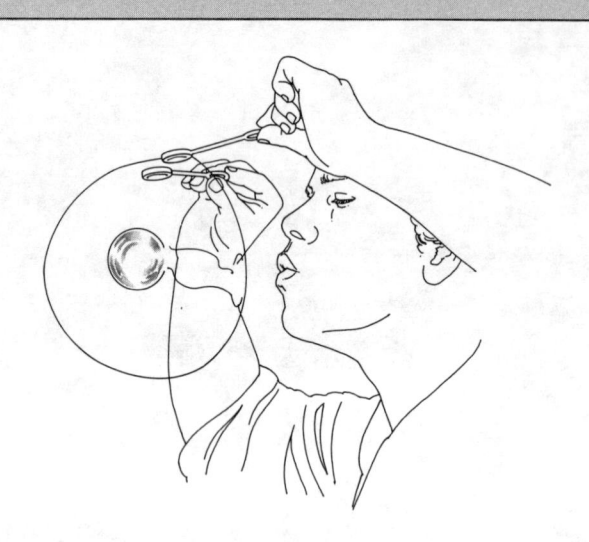

1. Blow a bubble that is at least apple-sized (grapefruit-sized will make it easier) and hold it up with two wands.

2. Get really close to it and pucker your lips as if you were going to whistle.

3. Aim at the equator (the middle of the bubble) and blow a quick, *short* puff of air.

   After you've got one inside, blow another, and another. Every time you add one, the outside bubble gets that much bigger, so you can never fill it up. The bubbles inside bounce against each other and against the walls, sometimes joining together or joining with the mother bubble, blipping out, popping, exploding, imploding, and who knows what all.

## PROBLEMS?

*●You blow, but the bubble just pops.*

Maybe you blew too hard. If the puff of air is a very small burst, you won't have time to build up to a hard blow. Some people are able to get it by making a "p" sound, but you'll disturb the bubble less if you just use your breath without closing your lips.

It could be that you blew the bigger bubble into your hand, or that it swung back and popped on your face. Try to blow straight at the equator and then move your head back out of the way.

The other possibility is that you took too long and the bubble thinned and was too fragile for this treatment.

*●You blow, but the bubble just blows off the wands.*

You probably blew too long a breath. It should be a sharp little quick breath that hits the bubble wall. The air should arrive at the bubble as a small packet, not a long tube.

*●The bubble shakes, but nothing happens inside.*

It could be that you didn't blow hard enough; bubbles aren't as fragile as we sometimes think.

It also could be that your aim is off. Aim at the equator and blow straight in.

# GOOD CLEAN FUN: BACKYARD AND BATHTUB BUBBLES

Here are some easy ways to make incredible bubbles with simple equipment.

## HOMEMADE JUICE

*1 cup warm water*

If your tap water is "hard," you'll do better with distilled or rainwater.

*1 tablespoon dishwashing liquid*

(I've had the best luck with Dawn, the blue kind, but others might work as well.)

*Optional: 1 tablespoon glycerin*

Most dishwashing liquids contain glycerin. Adding a little

more might help, but too much will just add weight and make things goopy.

Or, instead of glycerin, try adding some commercial bubble juice to this watery mixture.

Slowly stir this mixture, trying to avoid making suds. Warm water will make it easier for the soap to go into solution, but the juice will work fine at room temperature. If it gets cold, it may not work as well.

## BATHTUB BUBBLES

You don't need a wand to blow bubbles.

Try this in the bathtub: Get your hands wet and soapy, make a circle with your finger and thumb, and dip your hand into the juice to fill the circle with a sheet of soap film. Blow bubbles, catch them, stretch them, and bounce that bag of air back and forth between your hands. Try using two hands. Try inserting your wet hand or arm right into a bubble!

With your hands or a bubble wand or a straw you can build bubble dome structures on the side of the tub, on the water, on your tub toys, or on your own body.

## WHALE-SIZED BUBBLES

Homemade bubble solution is great for making giant bubbles because it's weaker than commercial brands. Dime store bubble juice is too strong (therefore, too slow) to make really big bubbles. You'll need a lot of juice for these bubbles—and remember, whales are fun, but they're too messy to play with in the house.

Increase the ingredients of Homemade Juice to:
*1 gallon warm water*
*1 cup dishwashing liquid*
*Optional: glycerin (up to 1 tablespoon) or lots of commercial bubble juice*

If you just want to *blow* bubbles, you can use your hands, a straw, a tube, a commercially-made bubble wand, a

*Beginning Bubbles*

homemade pipe-cleaner wand (see page 14), or a device of your own invention. But to quickly get enough air to make a really big bubble, you want to be able to *wave* a big sheet of film through the air.

There are bubble toys designed to do just that, but you can make your own. You'll need:

*3 feet of string*

This must be made of a material that will stay wet. Cotton is good, jute is fine, and even wool yarn works, but nylon isn't so good.

*2 plastic drinking straws*

Thread the string through both straws. Tie the ends of the string together. You now have a loop of string with two straw "handles."

Roll up your sleeves and wet your hands in the bubble juice (remember, dry fingers break bubbles). Holding one handle in each hand, dip the whole loop into the juice.

Keeping the handles together, lift them out of the juice and hold them up in front of you at waist height. Now pull the handles apart. You should now have a sheet of soap film.

*Pull* the loop through the air upward or sideways. (If you push, the bubble will break on your body.) When you want to close the bubble, just bring your hands back together.

You can run with this loop and make long tube-shaped bubbles that break off into spheres or just break; you can make big "S" shapes, and you can make spirals. I've sometimes been able to get a doughnut shape, but only very briefly; this is an unstable form that collapses on itself (sometimes trapping the air from the doughnut hole into a bubble that is itself trapped inside the bigger bubble). With very little pressure inside them, these big bubbles are so fluid that you'll be able to see them take some incredibly distorted shapes as they vibrate, stretch, undulate, wobble, and wooble around in the air.

If you dip a hula hoop into a plastic wading pool of juice, you might be able to put yourself inside a bubble, but this takes several gallons of juice and is very difficult to do if there is any wind.

# BEYOND ROUND BUBBLES..................

If you think of bubbles as being round, take a closer look at the soapsuds in the sink next time you're washing the dishes. The bubbles on top have rounded surfaces that bulge up into the air, but even these bubbles join their neighbors at sharp angles. The bubbles below the surface look more like faceted jewels. Whenever two bubbles touch, they join to share a common wall. You can read more about this on page 80, but with this chapter you can apply this simple fact to make more and more complex shapes.

# WIGGLY WORMS

These wiggling little worms are pretty easy to make, and they can be lots of fun.

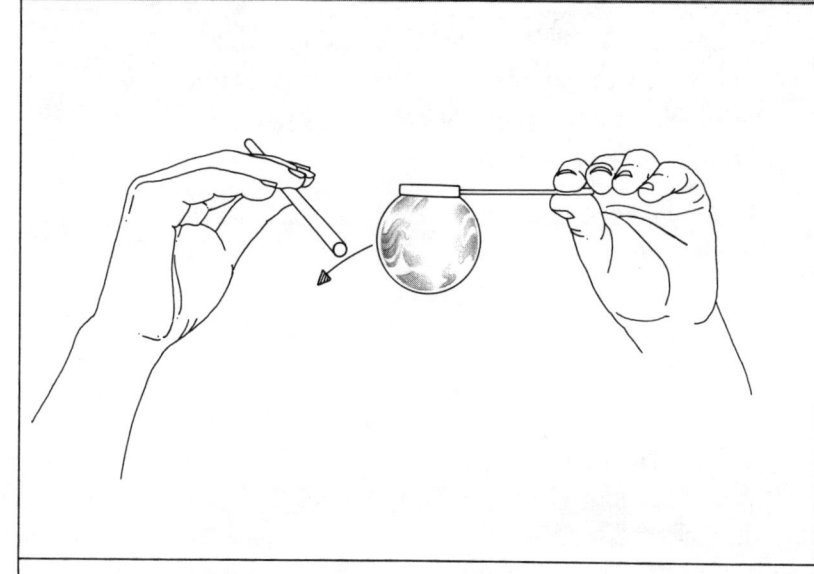

1. If you're right-handed, hold a straw in your right hand and a wand in your left. (I use my right hand to do most of the work. This means that I always blow bubbles through the straw or wand that I'm holding in my right hand. The wand in my left hand is used only to hold up bubbles and help guide them. If you're left-handed, just reverse these directions.)

With the straw, blow a small bubble onto the bottom of the wand. To detach the straw, swing it away quickly. (For tips on using a straw, see page 15.)

2. Touch the straw to the bottom of that bubble and blow a second bubble about the same size.

*Beyond Round Bubbles*

3. Add a third bubble, making sure that neither the straw nor the new bubble touches the first bubble.

Add as many more bubbles as you can, being careful that each new bubble touches only the bottom bubble on the growing worm. The more bubbles you add, the more the worm will wiggle.

## PROBLEMS?

*You blow a small bubble, but when you pull the straw away the bubble follows.*

If you move too slowly or if you pull the straw straight back, the straw will haul the bubble along with it.

First draw the straw back so that only its tip is touching the bubble, and then quickly swing the straw down and away to suddenly break contact.

*The separate segments keep joining together and forming suds!*

That happens only when bubble #3 and bubble #1 (or #4 and #2, or #5 and #3) touch each other. They can be joined by a wet straw or a wet wand, and they can join if the bottom bubble slides up along the bubble that separates them. Be careful to let only the tip of the straw touch only the bottom bubble. You can keep #3 and #1 farther apart if you make #2 bigger.

*The whole thing is too heavy, and it pulls apart or falls off the wand.*

Weight is the limitation on these worms, so don't dip the straw into the juice between blows; that will add another heavy drop to the bottom. You may even want to drain the drop at the bottom once in a while by touching it with the straw (but be sure to use a quick swing to detach the straw).

There is such a small area of contact between any two of these little bubbles that they can't support a very long chain, but it's fairly easy to hold up five or six little bubbles.

When you can make a Wiggly Worm with eight segments, you might want to try your hand at the more difficult Caterpillar (see page 68).

# THE BUBBLE CUBE

I once demonstrated Bubble Magic as part of a mathematics lecture at the University of California at Santa Cruz, and as I was planning my talk I told a friend of mine, who was a physics major there, that I was going to demonstrate a Bubble Cube.

My friend and I had had many conversations about the physics of soap films, and he recalled from his reading that "bubbles are minimal surface structures, that they always pull into the smallest, most economical form possible" and that "of all the shapes, the sphere is the most economical form in nature, using the smallest amount of surface to enclose a given volume."

Both those statements are true, but my friend's conclusion

*In this bubble, and in some other bubbles I make when I perform, I've used smoke to show the shape of the bubble. When you blow your own bubbles, you can easily see everything without the smoke; smoke isn't necessary to create any of the bubbles in this book.*

*If you want to see something interesting, blow bubbles outside when it's so cold you can see your breath; you'll see your warm breath inside the bubbles.*

—that a bubble cube is impossible—is false. The real world is more complicated than a couple of laws of physics, and even Einstein once said that his theory of relativity may prove to be only a "local phenomenon."

The Bubble Cube does not violate the known laws of physics. In fact, it is a beautiful demonstration of some of those laws. (For a discussion of how it works, turn to page 80 in "Fizzix.")

Here's what to do: First you'll blow two bubbles, and while holding that double bubble with a wand, you'll encircle the junction between the two with four more bubbles about the same size. Then you'll insert a straw into that cluster of six bubbles. When you blow through the straw, a bubble will emerge in the center of the cluster. A bubble surrounded on six sides by similar-sized bubbles will have to be a cube.

1. Dip the wand and the straw deep into the juice. Hold up the wand in one hand, and with the straw, blow a bubble onto the bottom of the wand. That's going to be the top bubble.

*Tom Noddy's Bubble Magic*

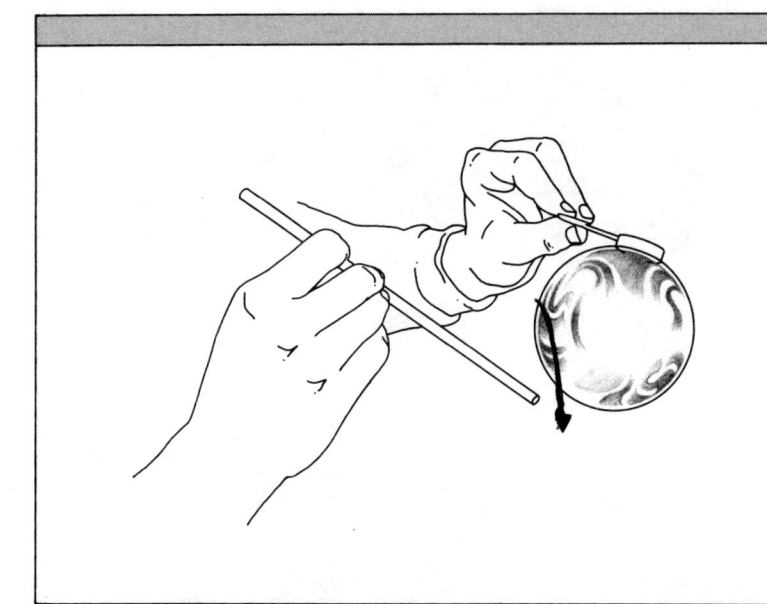

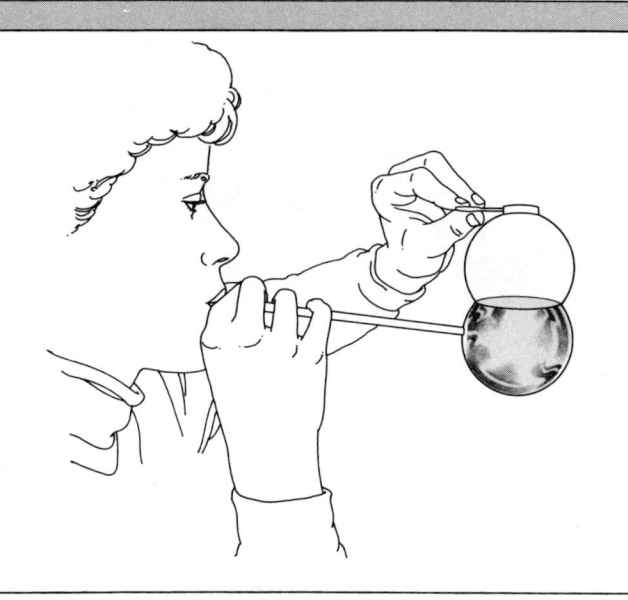

2. Remove the straw from the bubble by swinging it away with a quick jerk to the side. (Don't pull it, or the hanging bubble will follow you.)

3. Now touch the bottom of the bubble with the straw and blow a second bubble about the same size. This will be the bottom bubble. Swing the straw free.

*Beyond Round Bubbles*

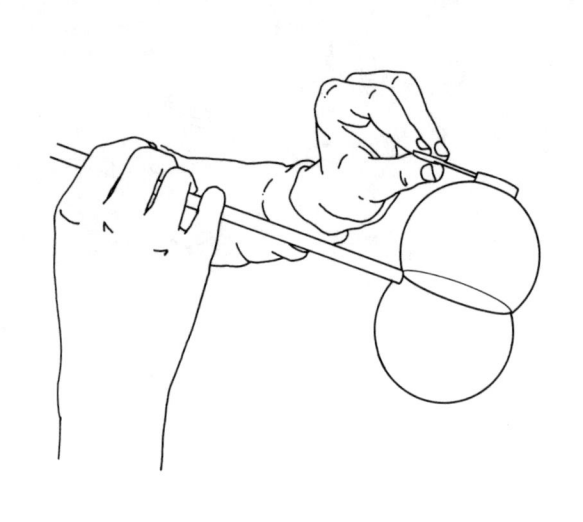

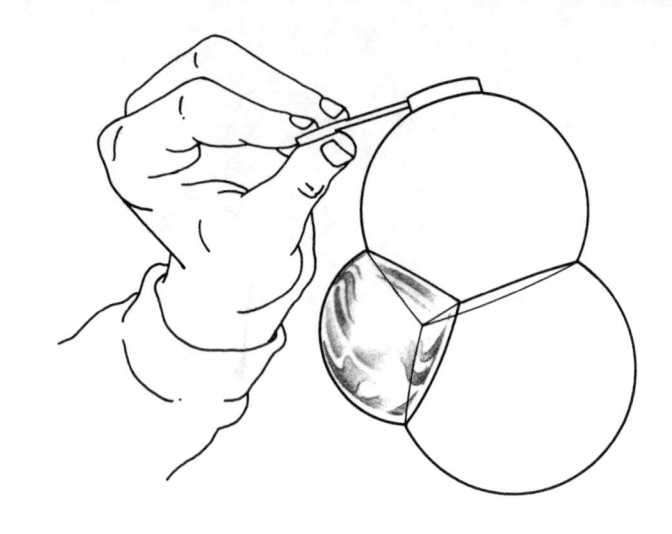

4. Focus your attention on the outside edge of the wall that divides the two bubbles. You are going to encircle that "neck" with a "necklace" of four large bubbles. If each of those bubbles is as large as the first two, the cube will be perfect, but I have to admit that I often make these four bubbles somewhat smaller. It's more important that these beads of the necklace be similar in size to each other. (Remember that if it isn't perfect, you can always use the straw to suck out or blow in some air to fix a bubble or two afterward.)

Touch the straw to the junction where the two bubbles meet. Don't insert the tip of the straw between the two; let it rest along the outside edge.

5. Blow the first bead for the necklace. Try to make it cover about one-quarter of the neck.

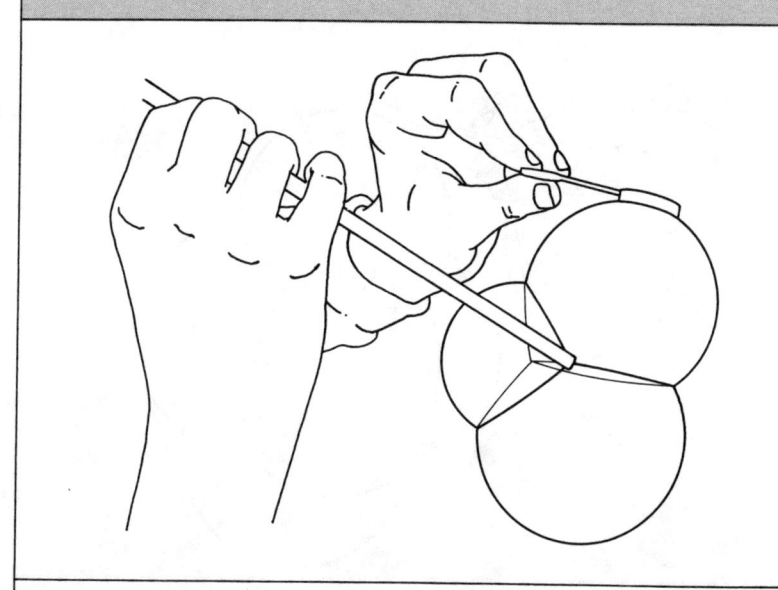

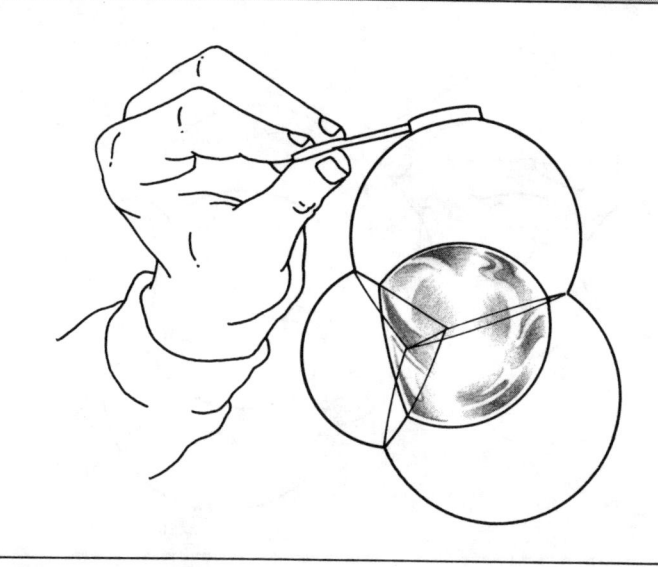

6. Swing the straw away from the bubble. You may need to dip the straw into the juice before you put it back in position on the junction. Just touch the end of the straw to the spot where you want the new bubble to grow (in contact with the neck and the first bead of the necklace).

7. Blow a second bead about the same size as the first, and quickly swing away the straw to break contact.

*Beyond Round Bubbles*

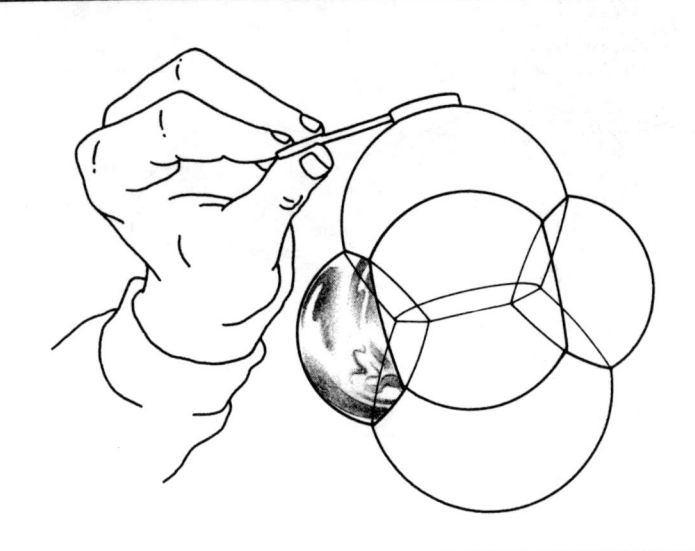

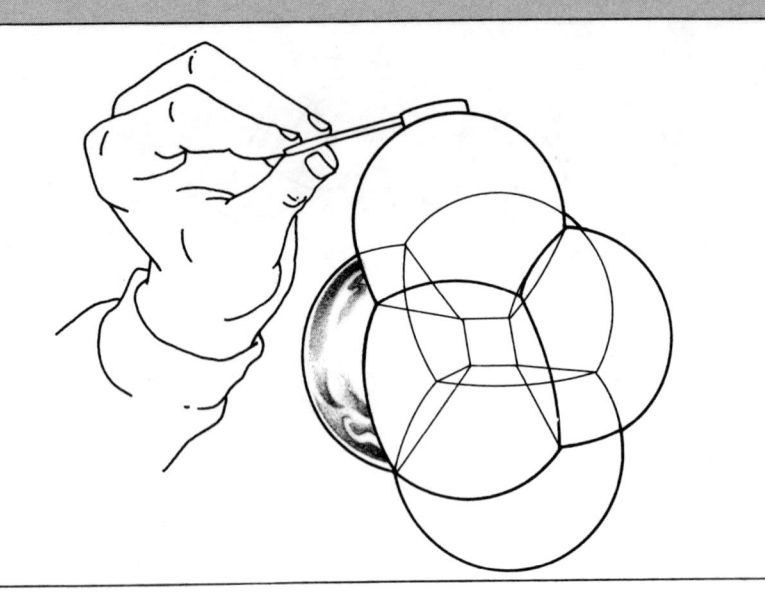

8. Reposition the wand at the junction, blow another bubble about the same size, and then swing away the straw just as you did before.

9. Reposition the wand at the junction, blow a fourth bead about the same size, and remove the straw.

You should now have a cluster of six bubbles about the same size, and in the center you should be able to see a sheet of film in the shape of a rounded square.

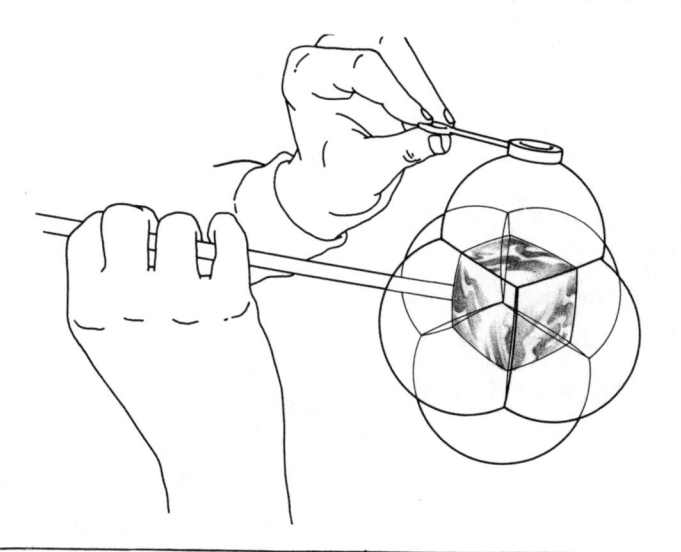

**10.** Now slide the straw in toward the center of the cluster. Don't worry about aiming it too carefully, because there is only one stable place in there for a bubble to be, and the new bubble will find that place. Now gently blow a bubble, and withdraw the straw.

The new bubble that has grown inside the cluster is surrounded by six bubbles. If those six bubbles are all equal-sized, they're all pushing in on the new bubble with equal force, so the new bubble *must* become a cube. (If I could push *you* hard enough equally from six different directions, you'd be a cube, too!)

Look closely at this shape. I have friends who call this a square bubble, but a square is a shape with only two dimensions. Some scientists are talking about the possibility that we may live in a universe of 11 dimensions; I don't know about *that*, but I do know that we live in a world that's at least three-dimensional. This bubble has length, width, *and* depth, so it's not a square–it's a cube.

It's not even a square cube; the six walls all bulge out from the center like the curved sufaces of spheres. The Bubble Cube is a lovely compromise between a cube and a sphere– a spherical cube.

*Beyond Round Bubbles*

## PROBLEMS?

*After you blow two or three bubbles, they start popping, even though you're careful to avoid touching them with a dry finger.*

The straw doesn't hold as much juice as the wand, so you need to dip it into the juice more often. If you dip it too often, the structure becomes heavy from all the extra juice. Dip after about every third bubble, more often on a dry day.

*After making the last bubble in the "necklace," it doesn't reach all the way around the "neck," and there is no square plane inside the cluster.*

Go ahead and insert the straw between two of the other bubbles and blow slowly. The growing cube will force the structure to close.

*You have the cluster of six, but when you insert the straw to blow the cube, something pops.*

The straw could be dry an inch or two from the end. Dip deeper into the juice. The other possibility is that it took too long to construct the cluster and the first bubbles have grown too old. Try again; you'll get quicker at this after a few tries.

*You have the cluster of six, but when you insert the straw to blow the cube, the bubble jumps out and forms a seventh bubble on the outside of the cluster.*

The straw wasn't inserted far enough (or it was inserted too far, right through to the other side). Another possibility is that you blew the final bubble too big.

The center is a very stable place for a bubble to be, and once it gets started there, it will stay there unless you blow it so large that it outgrows the cluster and reaches the outside. If it gets out of the center of the cluster it will jump to the outside and stay there, and it might even pop from the sudden stress of the jump.

# THE CAROUSEL

This is one of the most beautiful and most active bubble forms. It's also surprisingly easy to make.

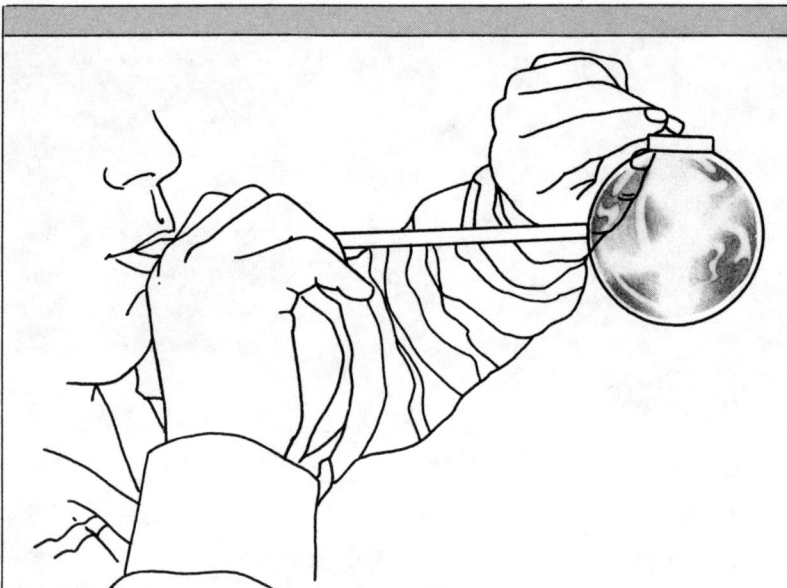

1. Blow two equal-sized bubbles that hang from the bottom of one wand, just as you did when starting the Cube.

*Tom Noddy's Bubble Magic*

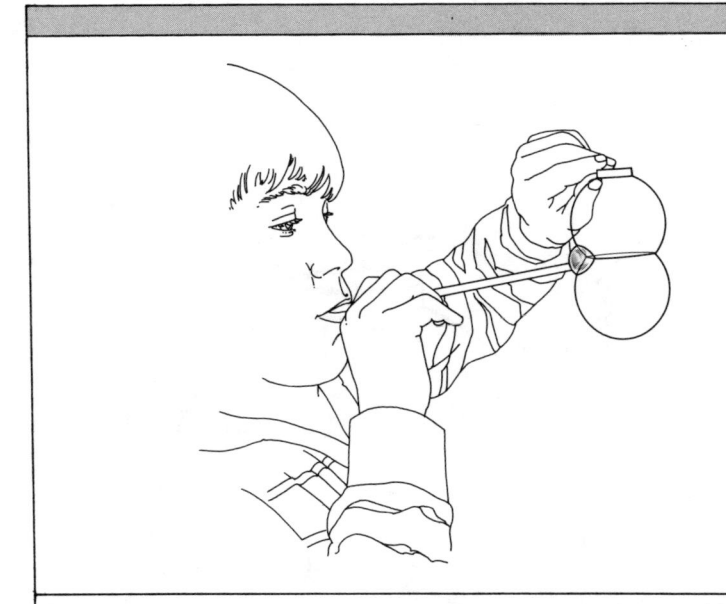

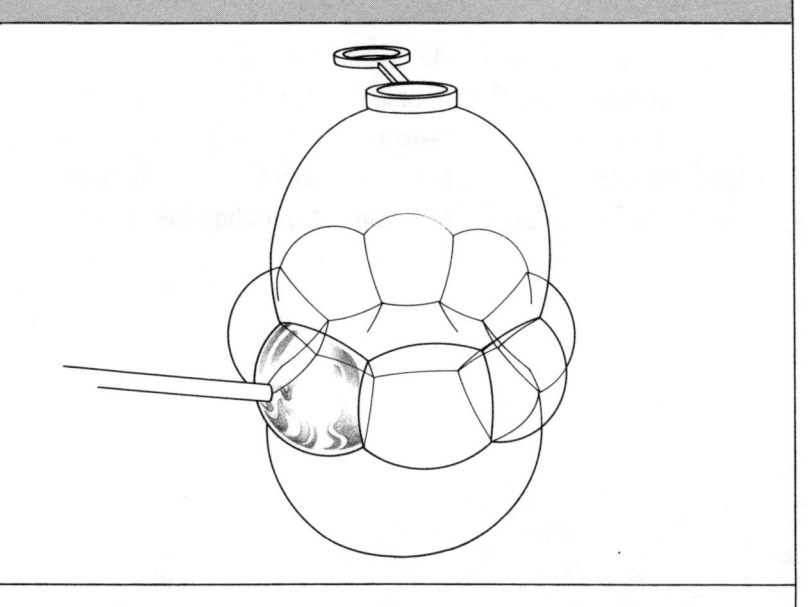

2. As you did for the Cube, place the tip of the straw at the junction between the two bubbles and begin to make a necklace of bubbles. This time, it really will look like a necklace because you'll blow much smaller bubbles.

3. Continue to add little "necklace" bubbles until you have surrounded the neck. The total number is not important (I usually end up with eight or nine), but the more the merrier. It is more important that they all be of similar size.

4. Now put the straw inside, just as you did for the Cube, and gently blow another bubble that will fill up the center of the carousel, forming a prism shape. (If you blew six "necklace" bubbles, it will be a hexagonal prism; eight will cause the inside bubble to take the shape of an octagonal prism.)

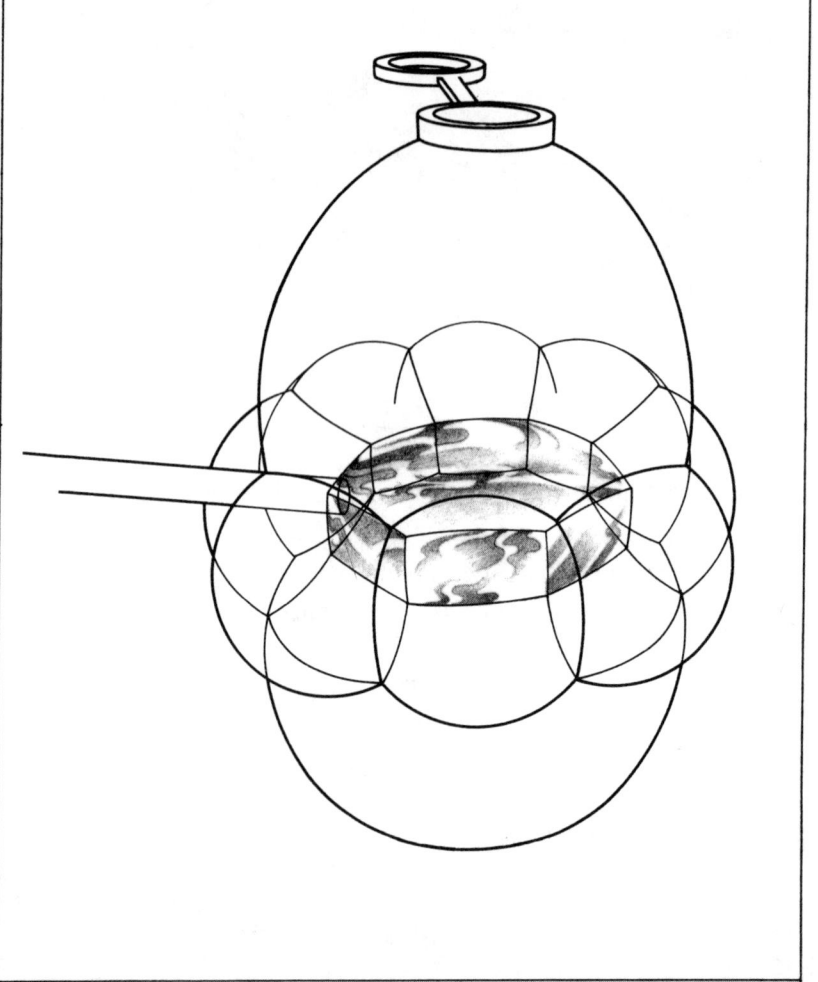

*Tom Noddy's Bubble Magic*

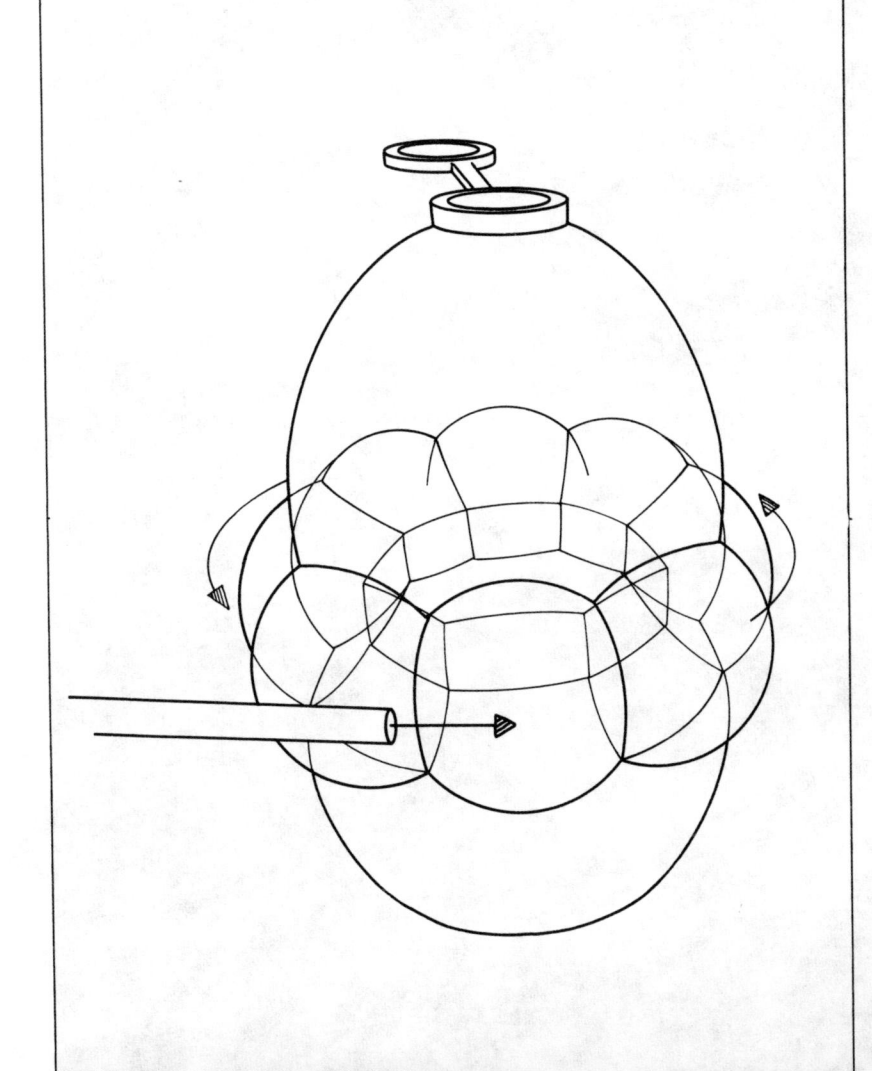

5. Now withdraw the straw and blow or suck air through it to remove any last film.

Blowing through the straw, aim a stream of air along the outside edge of the row of little bubbles. The whole structure will rotate like a merry-go-round.

## PROBLEMS?

Most of the problems you might have with the Carousel are the same as for the Cube (see page 52).

- *You are able to get the "necklace" all around, but when you try to inflate the center, you get multiple bubbles instead of just one.*

  Don't try to center the straw on that large film between the two large bubbles. Let the straw also touch the inside wall of the necklace before you gently blow.

- *You build the structure and inflate it, but you can't get it to spin.*

  You want the airstream from the end of the straw to just glide over the outer edge of the "wheel" of necklace bubbles. Start by blowing gently and then try increasing the speed.

*Beyond Round Bubbles*

# THE JEWEL

The Bubble Jewel is precious—and, according to Pythagoras, sacred. The shape is called a regular dodecahedron, one of the forms that the Pythagoreans referred to as the "five sacred solids."

Pythagoras was a Greek mystic who lived in the sixth century B.C., and he was one of the founders of Western mathematics. To Pythagoras and his followers, mathematics was a religion; they believed that the perfection they found in numbers, music, and geometry were reflections of a rational divinity whose laws could be discovered.

One of the things that the Pythagoreans discovered is that of all the three-dimensional forms possible, you can build only five that are made up entirely of identical faces with identical dimensions joined at identical angles. One of these is a cube: a cube is made of six equal squares, all joined at equal angles. The perfection seen in this shape appealed to the Pythagoreans, and to them it represented earth. The regular tetrahedron (four equal triangles joined at equal angles) represented fire. The regular octahedron and icosahedron (eight and 20 equilateral triangular faces, respectively) represented water and air. (Oddly, these are the two that bubbles won't form.)

And so the fifth sacred solid represented something beyond the four elements of earth, air, fire, and water. The regular dodecahedron (12 pentagons) was regarded as so sacred that it was a punishable offense to show this form to someone who had not been initiated into the cult of the Pythagoreans. (Since this cult died out about 400 B.C., I've decided to take a chance and not only show one but actually describe the method of constructing this beautiful and precious jewel. But don't tell any Pythagoreans where you found out, OK?)

Just as you did for the Cube, you're going to first build a cluster of bubbles that will determine the shape of the final bubble in the center. Since a cube has six equal faces, you started by making six equal bubbles. A dodecahedron has 12 faces, so this time you'll begin by making a cluster of 12 bubbles.

1. Begin just as you did for the Cube, by blowing two equal-sized bubbles joined together and hanging from one wand.

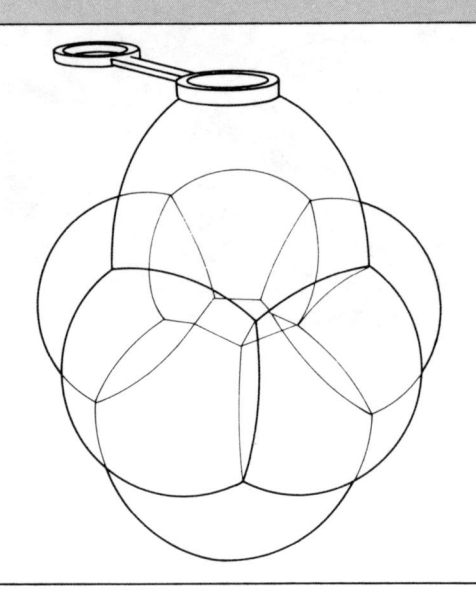

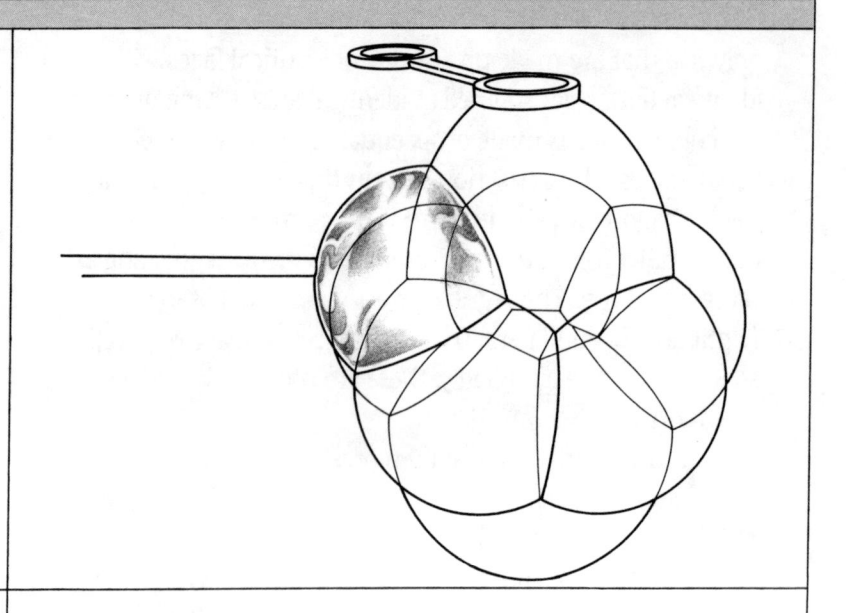

2. Blow five slightly smaller, equal-sized bubbles around the junction between the two bubbles.

3. Now add another row of five bubbles above the first "necklace."

To do this, place the straw at the outside junction where one of the "necklace" bubbles meets the top bubble. Blow a bubble here that is slightly larger than the lower "necklace" bubbles.

*Tom Noddy's Bubble Magic*

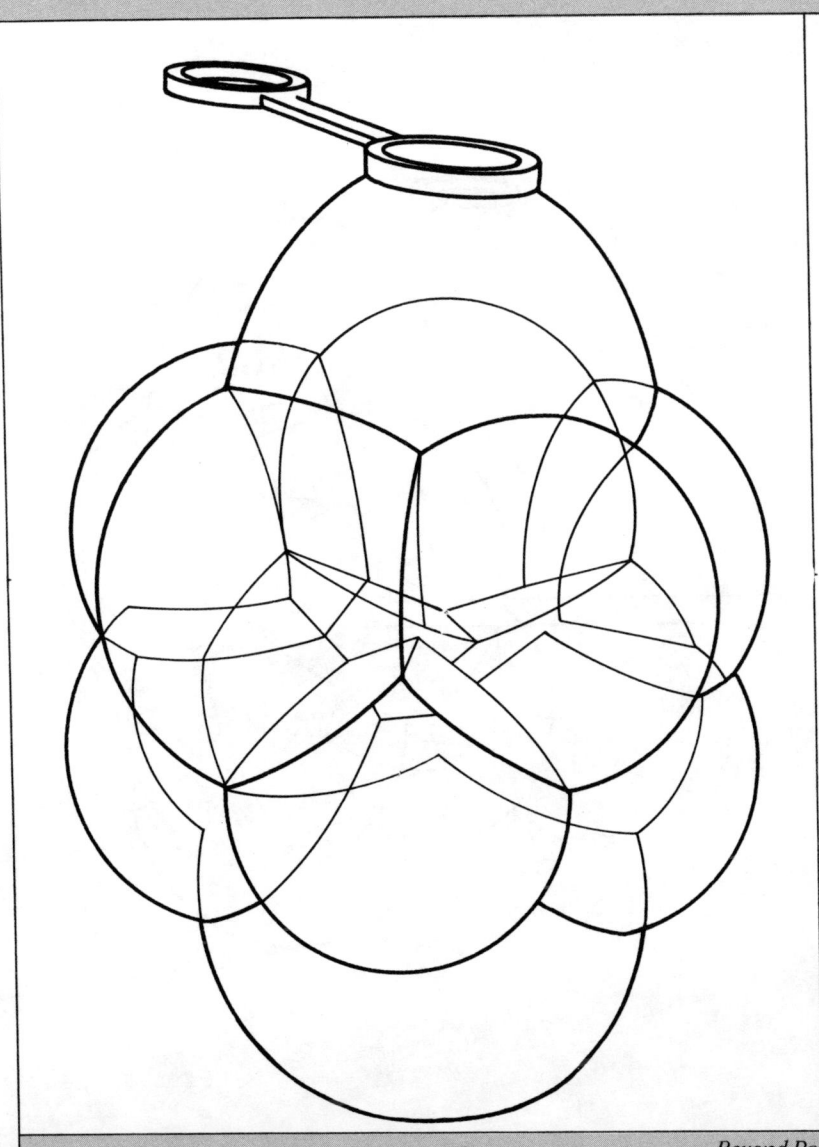

4. Now do the same for each of those other four junctions until you have a second row of five bubbles. This gives you a total of 12 bubbles in a symmetrical cluster.

5. Just as when you blew the cube, put the straw inside the cluster and gently blow a bubble. It will grow inside that cluster into a bubble that has 12 faces, each one shaped like a pentagon.

*Beyond Round Bubbles*

Using this same method of blowing a cluster of bubbles and inflating a bubble in the center, you can create some exquisite geometrical forms. By varying the size and number of bubbles in the cluster, I've been able to make bubble versions of the tetrahedron, cube, dodecahedron, numerous prism shapes, a truncated tetrahedron, a truncated cube, a truncated octahedron, and a shape whose name is "the great rhombicuboctahedron." There are mathematical limitations (see page 80), but the possibilities are enough to keep a person busy for quite a while.

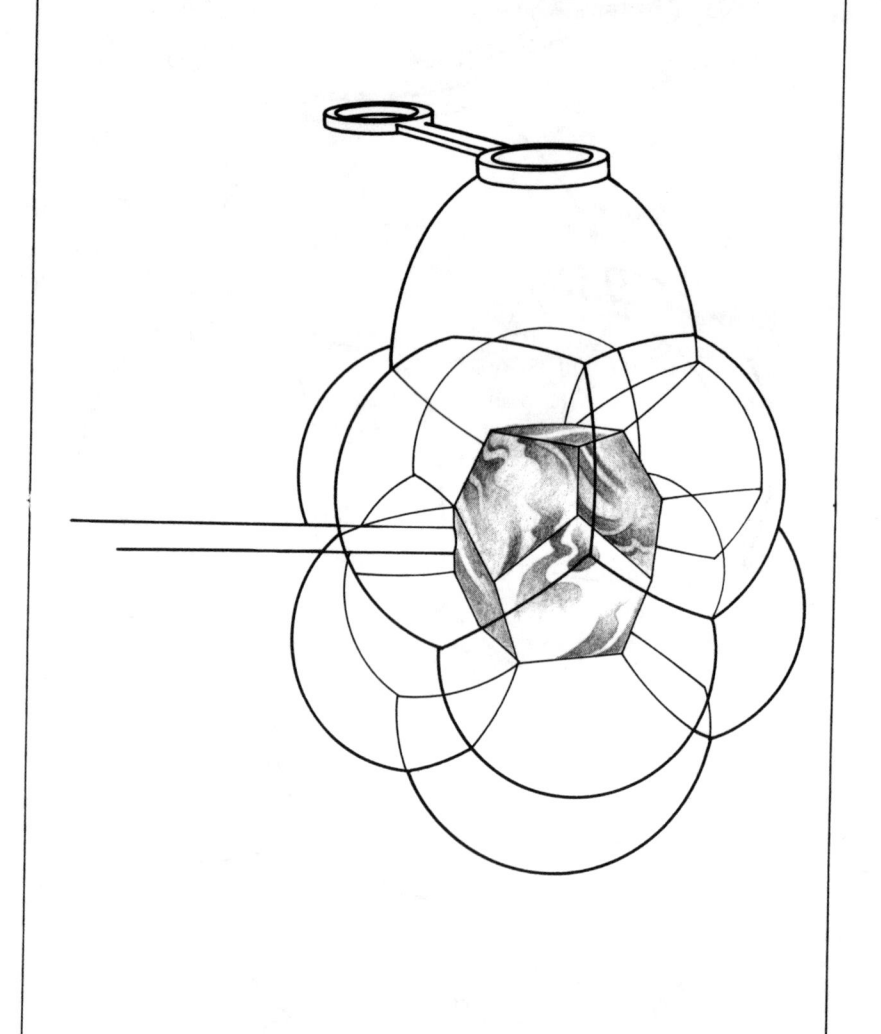

*Tom Noddy's Bubble Magic*

# PROBLEMS?

Many of the problems you might have with the Jewel are the same as for the Cube (see page 52).

• *After you blow four "necklace" bubbles, they join and there is no room for a fifth.*

Either you made them too big, or the original two bubbles are too small. If the first two (top and bottom) bubbles are small, you'll have to make very small "necklace" bubbles to fit five around.

• *You are able to get the first necklace all the way around, but there's a gap in the upper necklace, even with five bubbles.*

This upper necklace needs to be made of bubbles that are slightly bigger than the bubbles below, or they won't reach all the way around. A small gap probably won't matter; try blowing the Jewel inside anyway, and the gap will probably close as the Jewel grows.

If the necklace isn't close to being closed as you blow the last "bead," try blowing the last bubble too big until it reaches around to touch the next bubble. Then you can suck some air out to bring it back down to a reasonable size.

• *When you blow the upper necklace, one of the bubbles slips down to the level below, leaving you with a lower necklace of six bubbles.*

This happens when one or more of the bubbles on the lower necklace is a bit too small. Next time, make the lower necklace of bubbles bigger.

If you want to keep working with the same structure after this happens, touch the wall between two of the lower bubbles with the end of the straw and suck a little bit to break that wall (see page 34). That will give you five bubbles on the lower necklace. You might want to suck out a little bit of the air so that this bubble isn't so much bigger than the others.

# COSMIC BUBBLES...............

These bubbles require more patience and finer skills. But now that you're able to work efficiently with two wands, you'll probably welcome the challenge.

# GALACTICA

Galactica is a little solar system of soap bubbles, and you can't help but be reminded of planetary rotation as you watch its silent spheres spin around inside the expanding universe of a large bubble.

If you can blow a big bubble and a bubble inside a bubble, you have the skills necessary for the Galactica.

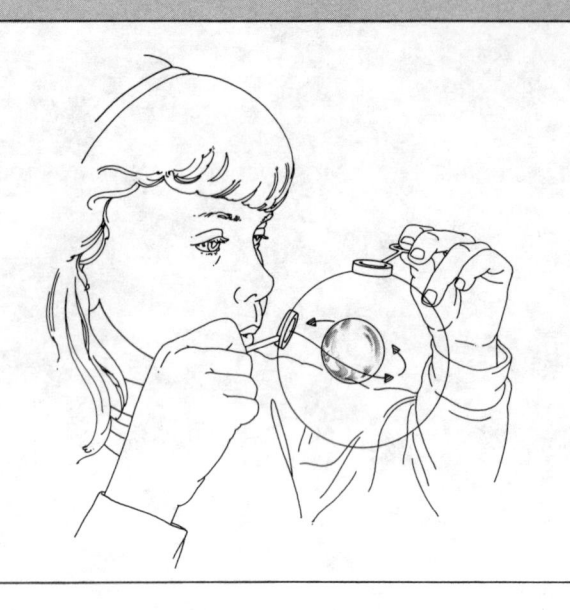

1. Using two wands, blow a big bubble.
2. Without closing the hole, move the wand that you've been blowing through away from your mouth, to one side, and quickly blow a bubble inside the bubble.

3. Quickly resume blowing through the wand into the bubble.

If the little bubble inside didn't blip out, it will begin to rotate inside, riding on the stream of air that is hitting the curved surface of the bubble.

You can continue as long as the big bubble lasts, adding more and more little bubbles, but keep returning to the wand to blow into the big bubble, or the inside bubbles will fall to the bottom and blip out while the big bubble deflates.

*Tom Noddy's Bubble Magic*

## PROBLEMS?

If you've successfully blown a big bubble and a bubble inside a bubble, you can learn to do both at the same time.

Don't be confused by the instruction to do things quickly. If you start with a bigger bubble, you have more time. Try that for a while till you get used to the movement.

- *The bubbles inside fall out and cling to the larger bubble at the bottom.*

They probably hit the bottom, where the gathering drop of juice was able to connect them to the larger bubble. Sometimes they hit one of the wet wands. There isn't much that you can do except to aim your blow along the inside edge of the large bubble to keep a good spin going. If you have lots of bubbles inside, some will probably blip out, so just put more in.

*Cosmic Bubbles*

# THE CATERPILLAR

You'll need two wands to build a Caterpillar, and when you finish, you'll need both wands to hold it up. These wands are the Caterpillar's antennae.

While the Wiggly Worm is built by adding bubbles to the bottom with a straw, the Caterpillar grows as you blow through the wand to add new bubbles to the top.

You can learn to have a real feel for bubbles if you practice building Caterpillars and dancing with them. The basic challenges are the same as those for the Wiggly Worm, but blowing through a wand instead of a straw means you have less control. It might take a while to learn the steps to this dance, but it's worth the time.

The big bubbles on a Caterpillar have plenty of room to

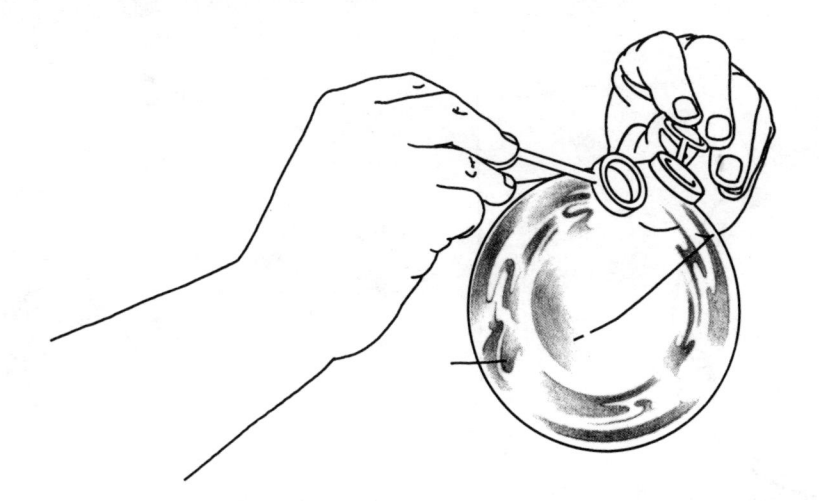

move. A gentle sway of the wands will generate a rippling wave motion through the chain of bubbles. It looks a bit like a breakdancer "doin' the Worm." A Caterpillar actually does the Worm better than the Wiggly Worm.

This form looks best when you have at least five segments. I usually make eight, but I've done as many as 18. Long Caterpillars are especially graceful.

1. Using two wands, blow a tangerine-sized bubble, and bring your right hand and wand to the top of the bubble as you flip the wand to close it (see page 20 for tips on closing a bubble).

2. This time, after you flip the wand to close the bubble, flip it back again to get into position to blow another bubble.

*Cosmic Bubbles*

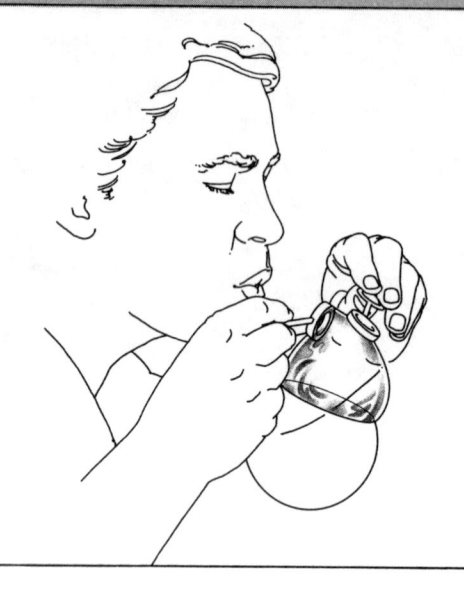

3. Keeping good contact with the top of the top bubble, tilt the bottom of the left wand toward you to receive the next bubble, and slide the right wand down on the bubble a bit.

4. Blow the next bubble through the right wand up onto the left wand. As the new bubble emerges, you can turn the left wand flat again to help hold up the structure.

*Tom Noddy's Bubble Magic*

5. Of course, you need to close that new bubble by flipping the wand over. When you turn this wand back again, you'll be ready to start the third (fourth, fifth....) bubble. The "old" bubbles fall down a notch each time, but they're still attached to the bottom of the new bubble as the structure grows from above.

Once you learn to do this quickly, the continual flipping motion of the wand will remind people of knitting.

## PROBLEMS?

• *Flipping the wand back and forth caused the whole structure to shake, and either it falls, or the bubbles cluster together into big suds.*

You don't need to take the wand off the bubble; it will slide along that liquid surface very smoothly, making only a little disturbance.

• *Alternate bubbles keep touching each other (as described on page 44).*

For a Wiggly Worm, you can carefully place each bubble at the bottom, but with the Caterpillar you must rely on the weight of the structure to pull the bubbles down while you add new bubbles above.

• *The weight seems to be too much and the whole Caterpillar pulls apart.*

Weight does limit the total number of segments, but if you make each new bubble slightly bigger, each one will have greater contact with the one below and will hold more weight.

That pendulum drop forming at the very bottom helps to anchor the structure, but it can get to be too much. If you give the Caterpillar a little shake, down and up, you can sometimes shake the big drop off, but be careful–too much of a shake and you won't be able to hold on.

*Cosmic Bubbles*

# THE LOVE BUBBLE

Love is one of the most difficult tricks. Two bubbles come together and become one! This actually happens fairly often in nature, and you may have accidentally caused the same effect while trying to do a different trick.

When two bubbles come together in the air they usually bounce off one another. Each has its own surface tension, and each surface has a slight positive electrical charge. Like two magnets with the same charge approaching each other, they repel without actually touching. To join them, we need a force greater than the force of this electrical repulsion. By swinging them together, we apply the kinetic energy of motion. In other words, to get love, you have to overcome surface tension.

Two bubbles become one? It seems absurd. If you were able to slam two oranges together to make one larger orange you would be rightly amazed. The spherical shape of a bubble reminds us of oranges and apples and balls, but remember that what we are dealing with here is liquid. You've often seen two raindrops come together on a windowpane, touch, and become one drop. You weren't surprised.

1. Blow two large bubbles, one on each wand, and hold them about 18 inches apart.

*Cosmic Bubbles*

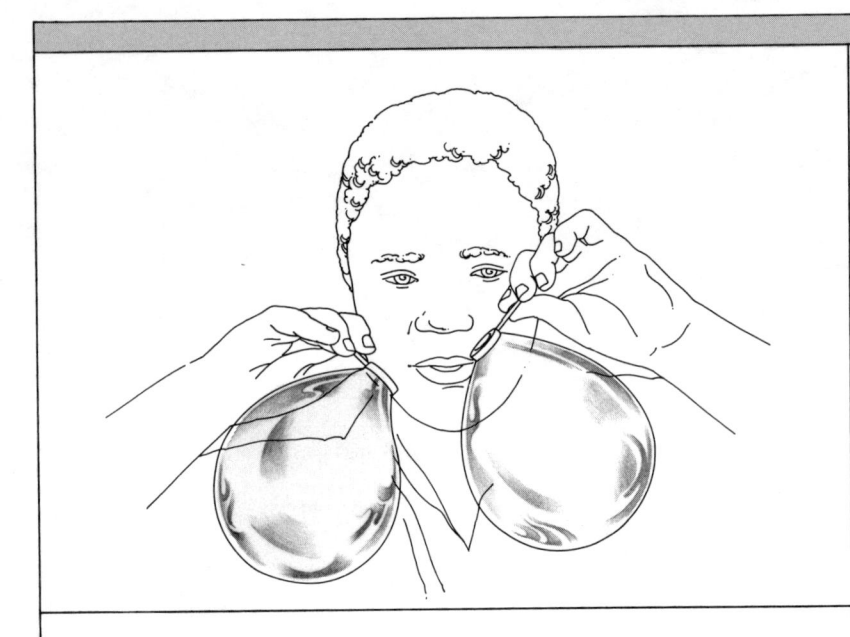

2. Tilt the two wands toward one another as you swing them toward each other, with the fat bubbles in tow.

3. Just before the wands touch, bring them both straight up to get them out of the way as the bubbles meet at the top.

*Tom Noddy's Bubble Magic*

# PROBLEMS?

◦ *The two bubbles bounce off each other.*

In fact, they didn't really touch; they bounced off an electrically charged cushion of air. Bring them together with a bit more force. This is easiest with larger bubbles. By towing the bubble along behind the wand, you create a "drag" on the film just below the wand. This thinner film meets its counterpart on the other bubble, and the force of impact actually breaks the walls, allowing the liquid of each bubble to flow into the other.

◦ *The bubble slips off the wand.*

Be sure to tilt the wand. The bubble should follow the "O" of the wand for maximum contact.

If you're tilting the wand, and the bubble still slips off, you could be moving it too suddenly. Try to tow the slippery sphere along smoothly.

If you shake the excess juice off the left wand before you blow the first bubble, it won't be as slippery.

The force is needed when the bubbles meet, not at the beginning of the swing. To build up speed more gradually, try holding the wands farther apart.

◦ *The bubbles break before you can swing them together.*

Maybe you took too long blowing the two bubbles, and they burst of natural causes (see "POP!," page 22).

Did one break on your hand? Don't let your hands follow in the bubbles' path.

Are both wands still wet? The circles and the stems?

◦ *As soon as the two got together, they broke up.*

Some couples do that. It's possible that you hit them together *too* hard, but more often the problem is that they were ready to burst. This will be a lot easier when you become faster at setting things up. In the meantime, it's a good sign that you were able to bring them together with such force.

◦ *They join as a double bubble instead of as one.*

This usually happens when the bubbles touch each other along the wet wand instead of joining bubble-to-bubble.

Try to get the wands out of the way at the crucial moment. This upward movement of the wands will also stretch the bubbles a bit more and make the imminent collision more dramatic. The impact must be great enough to break down the walls.

*Cosmic Bubbles*

# 5

# FIZZIX..................

Soap bubbles are so pure and simple, it's only natural that kids and physicists are their biggest fans.

The science of physics isn't mysterious. Our natural curiosity causes us to experiment with the world; when we were children, our experiments taught us to crawl, then walk, then run. We experimented with our toys to learn some basic rules of how the world works: rubber balls bounce, tops spin, blocks stack up, magnets stick together, magnets push apart, scissors cut paper, rocks break scissors.

The kids who became physicists are still experimenting, still looking for the basic laws. It shouldn't be surprising that they turn their attention back to the toys that were there when they first explored the workings of the world–including bubbles.

# Water

Ordinary water–$H_2O$–is a very dynamic combination of atomic elements. Each molecule of water is made of two hydrogen atoms (H) electrically attached to one atom of oxygen (O). Because the hydrogen atoms are attached to one side of the oxygen atom, a molecule of water is a bit lopsided, with one end mostly positive and the other end mostly negative.

This highly polar arrangement causes water molecules to act like little magnets: they stick to each other even while being poured. This electrical attraction brings the molecules together to form a liquid–water.

When you pour water from a bottle into a glass, the water molecules don't fly apart when they hit the air; they hold together in a stream as they fall. When the glass is filled to the rim, you can even add a little more water and it will bulge above the rim, held there by a force that keeps it from overflowing.

You can see this force even more dramatically in a drop of water that is slowly forming at the end of a faucet. The drop slowly gets bigger but still doesn't fall. Some force is acting *against gravity* to pull all of those water molecules *up*! That force is the electrical charge of the molecules themselves.

All molecules of pure water are created equal. They are made of the same kinds of atoms, they weigh the same, and they are equally attracted to each other. Yet in a glass of water, the molecules at the surface act very differently from the molecules below the surface.

A water molecule within the liquid is surrounded by other water molecules, and it is equally attracted to all of them. The effect of this equal pull in every direction is the same as no pull at all. But although the water molecule on the surface has water below and water at its sides, it has only the air above–and it is more attracted to other water molecules than to the air above. The sideways pulls cancel each other but the downward pull has no upward pull to counteract it; so all of the surface molecules are pulled down, away from the air. The effect on the liquid is much the same as if it had an elastic skin stretched over the surface, and this "skin" pulls inward and resists any effort to expand.

When this electrical force shows itself at the surface of a liquid, we call it *surface tension*. Every liquid has its own surface tension strength, which corresponds to the electrical attraction that its molecules have for each other. Water has the strongest surface tension of all the common liquids. This is one reason that bubbles of pure water can't last long: the molecular attraction of water is so strong and the molecules pull together with such force that the film collapses into drops.

# Soap

Did you ever wonder why we use soap to wash dishes? Soap is funny stuff; it has a split personality. One end of each soap molecule is attracted to water–it's hydrophilic.

The other end is hydrophobic—it doesn't like water.

Unlike soap, grease is completely hydrophobic. You know what happens when you pour grease into water: it beads up, floats to the surface, and does everything that it can to pull away from the water.

If you pour liquid soap into a sinkful of water, the end of each soap molecule that likes water attaches itself to a water molecule that holds the soap in solution. But what about the other end of that poor soap molecule? Everywhere it turns there's more water, and it doesn't like water. ("Oh, ouch...oh no, water!...ow, turn away, up there, oh no...ouch, *look out!*") How can it get away from the water? Well, bless your heart, if at this point you slide a greasy spaghetti plate into the soapy water, the ends of the soap molecules that don't like water will attach to grease molecules. Now the ends of the molecules that like water are attached to the water, and the ends that don't like water are attached to the molecules of grease, and you've just made a bunch of little soap molecules happy. If you wipe the plate a little, soap molecules can get underneath the grease and surround it and then you can float it away in that flood of water. That's why we use soap to wash our dishes.

But before you put that greasy plate into the water, some of the soap molecules had already found a temporary solution to their dilemma. If you could drop one soap molecule into a glass of clean water, it would be buffeted about by the electrical repulsion of the water molecules until it found its way to the surface, and once there it would stay there. If you pour lots of soap into a glass of water, the soap molecules will cover the surface before any will stay submerged. At the surface, the water-loving ends of the soap molecules cling to the water below while their hydrophobic ends stick up into the air away from the water—another happy arrangement.

Something else happens when you add soap to that glass of water: the surface tension of the water decreases. Water molecules near the surface are separated by soap molecules, and at this greater distance their electrical attraction exerts less force. Since surface tension works to pull the surface inward, a decrease in surface tension will allow the surface area to enlarge. The pull of surface tension is still strong enough to hold the liquid together, but now the tension has relaxed enough to allow a greater stretching of the surface.

If you lift that surface liquid onto a ring and blow against it, you can see how truly flexible it is. But if you stop blowing, you'll see the force of surface tension working to reduce the surface area of the bubble back to a flat film.

A bubble made of pure water will soon collapse under its own surface tension (or from evaporation), but without some surface tension, the film couldn't exist—the molecules would fly apart. Mingled with soap, water provides the surface tension necessary to hold a bubble together, while the soap slows evaporation and increases flexibility.

# Pressure

The air inside a soap bubble is under pressure; it's being squeezed by the surface tension of the soapy water.

The force that surface tension exerts on a bubble is always the same; whether the bubble is thick or thin, large or small, surface tension squeezes the air inside with the same force. Yet when bubbles of two different sizes join, the wall between them bulges into the larger bubble. The greater the difference in their sizes, the greater the bulge.

Strange as it may seem, the pressure inside a small bubble is greater than the internal pressure of a large bubble. This might sound illogical because you may know that as you blow more air into a balloon (or bicycle tire), the air pressure becomes greater. But as you blow more air into a bubble, the internal pressure becomes less.

Soap bubbles are similar to balloons, but in many ways they are different. Both have air pressure pushing out, and both have a force pulling inward, but the surface tension of the bubble pulling in is quite different from the force of the stretched rubber of the balloon.

As a balloon fills with air, it gets bigger and the rubber resists further stretching with an increasingly greater force. An expanding bubble wall doesn't resist the incoming air with a greater force; instead, the force of surface tension remains the same, while the bubble gets bigger.

Pressure is the relationship between force and area, and when the same force of surface tension acts on an increasingly larger area, the result is less pressure. A large bubble exerts the same force on the air inside it as a small bubble–and so the air inside the large bubble has less internal pressure.

# Angles

Next time you're doing the dishes, look closely into the suds in your sink–but be careful; you could get lost in that random array of soapy structures. It looks as though *everything* is happening in that chaos: little apartments designed by a mad architect, a labyrinth of lines scattering in every direction, a switchback of soap film surfaces, a plethora of polychromic polygons and polyhedra, convexities, concavities, angles, edges, corners, and junctions. It's not what it seems.

A sightseeing tour deep into that maze is not recommended for the casual bubble tourist, and even the most intrepid explorers may have to double back now and then to get their bearings straight.

If you want to run ahead on your own, feel free. The following list of facts about bubble angles is a map that probably will make more sense after you've explored the maze for a while, and the suds may make more sense after you've browsed through the facts for a while. Don't let the numbers scare you; there aren't any in the real suds, and the map is not the territory. This is not a textbook, and there won't be a quiz. The numbers are accurate, but important only if you find them interesting.

# Suds

The apparent chaos in a sinkful of soap suds is, in fact, a very precise geometric network.

If bubbles are being blown or some are popping, other bubbles will be in motion, and they'll slide through different compositions, but when the movement stops, all the liquid lines and soap film surfaces will lock into this arrangement:

Wherever bubble *walls* meet, there are always three walls meeting along an *edge* (the lines that you see where three bubble walls meet), at three equal 120-degree angles; and,

Wherever edges meet, there are always four edges meeting at a *point* (vertex), and the edges meet at equal angles of 109 degrees, 28 minutes, 16 seconds.

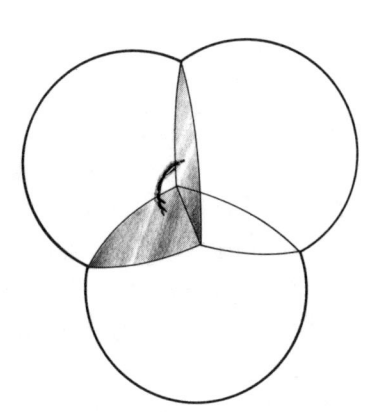

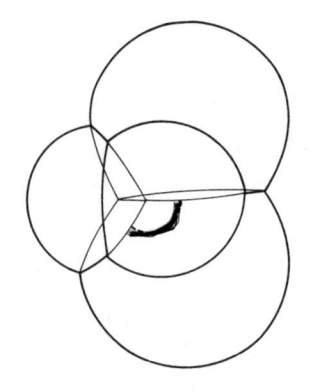

Walls meet walls and edges meet edges at identical angles, and they have met only at those exact angles in all the suds that there have ever been.

Having prepared ourselves for a major expedition, let's take a shortcut. In a simpler structure of larger bubbles, we can see all the major landmarks and be back in time for lunch.

Forget your backpack; all we need for this trip is some bubble juice, a straw, and a flat surface that we can get wet (a countertop, a plate, or a sheet of plastic). You'll be able to see the bubbles best if the surface is black or some dark solid color. Maybe you could cut or fold a section of a dark plastic garbage bag and lay it out on a flat surface.

We're just going to blow four bubbles down onto this surface and look at them.

1. Pour a little bubble juice onto the surface and use the straw to spread it around an area about the size of a dinner plate. Be sure not to leave any dry spots.

2. Next, wet the straw in the juice.

3. Touch the wet end of the straw to the surface and gently blow a bubble. Then take the straw away.

4. Blow a second bubble near the first and they will join, forming a double bubble with a wall between them.

If the bubbles are the same size, the wall will be flat. You can put the straw back into one of the bubbles and slowly suck out some of the air until it is noticeably smaller than the other. The greater pressure in the smaller bubble will cause the wall to bulge into the larger bubble.

*Tom Noddy's Bubble Magic*

5. Touch the straw to the outside edge where they meet, and blow a third bubble.

In the center you'll see that the three walls are joined at equal angles (even if the bubbles are different sizes).

6. Looking down from above, find the slight depression where the three walls meet. Touch the tip of the straw to that spot and gently blow a fourth bubble so that it rests on top of that pocket.

7. Look into the center of that cluster, and you'll see that the lines converge at a point. Four lines (edges) come together at equal angles to meet at one point (vertex).

When you added a fourth bubble, what effect did it have on the walls? Look along the lines: how many walls meet to form that line? I'm sure that you'll find no change; three walls are meeting along that edge, and four of those edges are meeting at a point.

You can add as many more bubbles to the cluster as you like, and you can divide the walls endlessly, but they'll always meet at the same angles. Some chaos, eh?

To sum up, the surface tension of soapy water is the force always at work trying to shrink the surface of a bubble. Only the compressed air inside a bubble stops that force from collapsing the bubble into a single round drop. The forces reach a compromise: the internal air pressure keeps the bubble inflated, but surface tension forces the bubble to assume a shape that minimizes the surface area.

Because a sphere is the most economical shape in nature, a single bubble in the air pulls itself into the shape of a sphere. When two bubbles touch, each will have a smaller surface area if they join to share a common wall, and so they do.

When three bubbles join, the most economical arrangement is for all three to join along an edge at equal 120-degree angles, and so they do.

When a fourth bubble joins that cluster, the most economical arrangement is for them to form edges where three walls meet, and a point where four edges meet at angles of 109 degrees, 28 minutes, and 16 seconds. And so they do.

## Colors

If you look at the bubble juice in a jar, you'll notice that it's a clear liquid (or, if it's colored, it's just one color). But a bubble blown from that same liquid and held in sunlight can display every color of the rainbow.

If the colors aren't in the liquid, where do they come from? Like all colors, the colors of bubbles are produced by light. The thin film of a soap bubble, held in the white light of the sun, can separate the light into its component colors, cancelling some of the colors, intensifying others, and reflecting an array of swirling iridescent patterns that correspond to the exact thickness of the soap film in any part of the bubble.

When you look at the colors of a bubble, you are looking at a contour map of the bubble's microscopic hills and valleys that can be measured in millionths of an inch. To understand how this is so, you'll need to know something about the nature of light.

The sun radiates waves of electromagnetic energy. Most of this energy is invisible to our eyes because the waves are either too long or too short to stimulate the "electrical antennae" in the retinas of our eyes (radio waves are too long and X rays are too short). Wave lengths are measured by the distance from one wave crest to the next, and the only energy waves visible to our eyes are those that measure between 15.5 millionths of an inch and 30 millionths of an inch. These are the waves of visible light.

Visible light is a continuous spectrum of colors. The longest waves that we can see are red. Next are yellow; the middle of our range is green; then cyan (blue-green); then blue; and then violet, the shortest wavelengths of visible light. In sunlight, all these waves stimulate our eyes at once, and the combination appears as white light. (If no light waves are acting on our eyes, we see nothing–black.)

Our eyes don't need all the colors of the spectrum to see white. A combination of long waves (red), some medium (green), and some short (blue) waves is enough for us to perceive white. Red, blue, and green are called the primary colors of light.

Early in school you probably learned how to mix the primary colors of paints–red, blue, and *yellow*–to produce any other color. You also can combine the primary colors of light (red, blue and *green*) to produce any color, but colors of light combine differently.

A white wall looks white because the paint on the wall is reflecting some of each color of light back to our eyes. If you shine a red spotlight on a white wall in a dark room, the wall will reflect only that color and the wall will appear red. If you add a blue light, the wall will reflect red and blue together and will appear magenta (red-blue). If you then add a green light, the wall will reflect all three primary colors and the wall will appear white.

Now suppose that you step in front of the red light so that only the green and blue reflect from the wall. When you see all three primary colors together, they combined to produce white, but when you interfere with one color (in this case, red) the color reflecting from the wall changes and appears cyan, a blend of green and blue.

Colors of light have opposites called complementary colors. Two colors are complementary if together they combine to produce white. For example, red and cyan (green-blue) are complementary, because combining them is the same as adding red to green and blue–the three primary colors that produce white. The complement of green is magenta (red-blue), and if you were to step in front of the green light instead of the red, the wall would reflect green's complement, magenta. If you interfere with the blue light, the

*Tom Noddy's Bubble Magic*

wall will appear as blue's complementary color—yellow.

A film of soap also interferes with some parts of white light to eliminate some colors and reveal others, but instead of physically blocking some of the light, the thin film causes some light waves to cancel others.

The colors we see in bubbles are produced by two sets of reflections—one from the outer surface of the film and one from the inner surface.

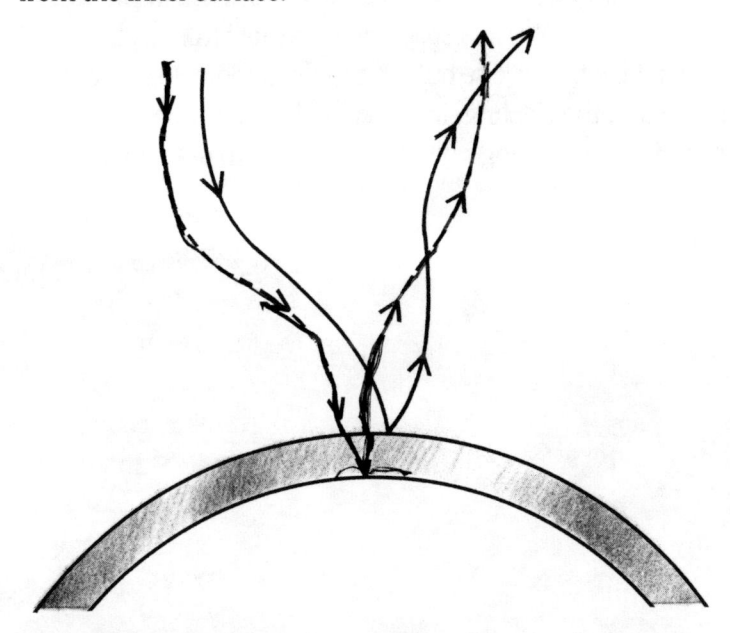

When sunlight strikes the outer surface of soap film, some of each color of light is reflected. Some of the remaining light waves that enter the film are reflected off the inner surface. As the reflections from the two surfaces return, waves of each of the colors meet. If all waves were to meet crest to crest and trough to trough, you'd see white light on the bubble. But whenever waves of the same length (for example, red) meet perfectly out of phase, the crest of one wave fills the trough of the other; then the red color is cancelled and you see its complement, cyan (blue-green). Where green is cancelled, the resulting color is magenta; and where blue is cancelled, the film looks yellow. (And where yellow waves meet yellow waves crest to trough, the bubble film appears blue.)

How do some of the light waves get out of step? The varying thickness of the soap film determines which wavelengths (colors) will meet out of phase and which meet in phase. Waves of light that enter the flowing liquid and reflect off its inner surface must travel a greater distance before they exit the film and head toward your eyes than light waves that simply bounce off the outer surface. How much farther these waves travel, and their position when they meet the other stream of waves, is determined by the thickness of the film they penetrate. A film exactly as thick as the length of a red wave will cause red waves that pass through it to exit perfectly out of step with red waves that merely reflect off the outer surface, and the two sets of waves will cancel one another.

On that area of the film, where red is cancelled by wave interference, we will see cyan—red's complementary color.

*Fizzix*

Where the width of the film is only ¾ the length of a red wave, two sets of red waves would not be perfectly out of step, but this might be the perfect thickness to cause a different wave length (such as blue) to be out of step. Wherever blues waves cancel one another, we see blue's complementary color—yellow. Where we see magenta on a bubble, we know that the film is the perfect thickness to cause green waves to meet out of step and cancel each other.

The fact that some colors seem brighter than others is the result of light waves of that color meeting in step—crest to crest. When two equal-sized waves meet in phase, they reinforce each other. This is also true of water waves or any other waves: water waves that meet in phase add their energy together to make one bigger wave with a taller crest and a deeper trough. When two equal-sized light waves meet in phase, the color we see is more intense. This kind of wave interference is called constructive interference, and it can be responsible for tsunami (tidal waves) or the brightness of the colors on a bubble.

Because of wave interference, we can see the whole spectrum of colors in a soap bubble created from a clear liquid. Like the precise but seemingly random structure of soap suds, the rippling, iridescent colors of a soap bubble reflect an ever-changing but orderly system of events.

# A MAGIC NATION.....................

As a child, I lived in my imagination—the magic nation that all children know. Some grownups leave that land, never to return, but others of us have learned to find our way back across its borders. The stories in this chapter tell of some of the travelers who have been my companions and my guides through this land.

# Eiffel

I heard about him from a magician. I was told that he was 80 years old, that he had been working with bubbles for over 50 years, that he had had a vaudeville act, was a professor of physics, and lived on a farm in southern Indiana. His name was Eiffel G. Plasterer. I was on the East Coast heading west. I called ahead, then dipped south.

When I pulled up to the farm, the sign said "Plasterer's Saw and Sorghum Mill, est. 1899." I found out later that that was the year Eiffel was born.

The trip to his farm had started to take on the feeling of a pilgrimage. I'd been doing my bubble act for nine years and had never met anyone who had spent more time with bubbles than I had. How could this guy be all these things? Eiffel sounded too good to be true, and I decided to prepare myself for disappointment.

It only took one look: no question, Eiffel G. Plasterer was the genuine article. He had a small frame that seemed to dart even while he moved slowly, pure white hair, a neatly trimmed goatee, and lines on his face that all said "Smile!"

He showed me around his farm: the steam process used to extract sorghum from cane and the distilled water byproduct that he uses in his bubble solutions, the collection of old steam-powered farm machinery that he and his son tinker into working order, the farm animals, and the apparatus he used for his vaudeville acts that he called Pendulums Fantasia and the mysterious "whirling lights."

I was anxious to see him blow bubbles, but after only a few heartbeats, I took a deep breath and allowed that his sense of pace was more appropriate than mine to the unfolding of his story.

While he was attending college, a professor had showed him how a sheet of soap film vibrates to form distinctive geometric patterns when sound waves from a loudspeaker are directed at it. "Oh, I thought that that was marvelous," he recalled; "I was actually *seeing sound*." This initial spark ignited in him an interest that would burn for the rest of his long life.

After college he became a physics teacher and developed his own soap solutions and bubble-blowing devices for classroom demonstrations. He took his family and large trunks of equipment on the road, touring the vaudeville and Chautauqua circuits with his "Bubbles Concerto" and "Pendulums Fantasia" shows, which he called the two great loves of his life. The pendulums act was just too "scientific" for the vaudeville audiences, he said, but "Oh, they *liked* the bubbles" ☼.

That glint that shot from his eye was intentional, but not false—not so much as if he put it on, but more as if he let it out. He used it for punctuation as he spoke, but occasionally it flashed out on its own.

He finished his story by remembering the college professor who first showed him science in soap films:

"After thinking about it, I said to the professor, 'You know, if a man knew what he was doing, he could do a whole *show* with bubbles.'

"But he said, no, there wasn't much that you could do with them. But I went on and I did…and Oh! I'm glad I did…" ☼ "…or you wouldn't have come here, would you?"

I took out my jar of bubbles, thinking that I'd start with something basic, a bubble inside a bubble, something that must have occurred to both of us. I blew a large bubble and then blew a short burst of air at the wall of the bubble. Now there was a bubble inside the bubble and I was prepared to go on to the next trick, but he was visibly startled. In over 50 years of playing with bubbles, he'd never seen them act that way.

"Oh, that's a very fast solution you have there," he said.

Since I always used the dime-store juice, I didn't know what he meant by "fast solution." Eiffel explained that he had formulated nine different solutions for his show. He referred to them as fast and slow, and he called his bubbles wet and dry, heavy and light.

His pace quickened, and he asked to see what else I could do, pausing only to call other members of his family over. He was delighted and delightful, graciously complimenting my skill while admiring my increasingly complex bubble forms. A few of the forms, it turned out, were ones he knew by other names; he knew how to make a Caterpillar but called it a Bubble Chain, and he performed the Love Bubble as the Marriage of Two Bubbles. Surprisingly, he wasn't able to do some forms with his stronger solutions, but those solutions made stronger bubbles that lasted longer and accepted quite different treatment.

Then he invited me down into the basement to see the bubbles he kept in jars: maybe a dozen big wide-mouthed glass jars capped with screw-on lids. Inside each jar was a bubble about the size of an apple, sitting on a little glass table that was glued to the bottom of the jar. Eiffel would wet this little table with some of the solution, dip the end of a rubber tube into the juice, extend the end of the tube down into the jar, and blow a bubble. He would then immediately screw on the lid. Some bubbles had color, and some were shiny silver orbs.

"This bubble," he said, "is over 100 days old. They're not very interesting the first 100 days; now, this one over here is 220 days old."

To produce this bubble, he had used his "Long-lived" solution, which produces very thick, or "slow," bubbles. When they are first blown, they are too thick to produce the wave interference patterns that let us see colors on a bubble.

As I gazed in amazement at the 220-day-old bubble, he said, "You can see that this has thinned down to the point where we can see the colors." They were the richest colors I had ever seen on a bubble–which is to say, the richest colors I have ever seen anywhere.

Over the months, as the liquid ran slowly down, he would watch his bubbles and record their progress. His oldest bubble was 340 days old! He explained it this way: the jar protected the bubble from dust, the dark cellar protected it from the evaporating effects of the sun, and the thick, viscous liquid drained so slowly that the top of the bubble held together throughout the 340 days.

One of the things that amazed me most about these bubbles is that they never popped. Every bubble that I've ever blown has popped. Eiffel explained that the air inside a bubble is under pressure; it wants to get out, and it can. Molecule by molecule, the air passes through the liquid surface, and the bubble shrinks into a puddle of liquid. When the bubble is gone, the liquid that remains can be used to blow another bubble. Eiffel told me that once he looked at one of those puddles under a microscope and saw the bubble, still shrinking.

With his mysterious bubble solutions, his odd bubble-blowing devices, tanks of hydrogen gas, vials, and jars, Eiffel G. Plasterer looked like a wizard, a scientist, a sweet eccentric working his scientific magic.

Before we left, I asked him a technical question, something about his formula or technique, and as he turned to look at me he asked, "Are you asking me as a magician or as a scientist?"

Unprepared (never having asked myself the question), I stammered, "Oh—as a, uh…as a…as a scientist."

"Well then," he said, "I'll have to tell you everything, won't I?" ☼

# The Bubble Brat

What a brat! He wouldn't take turns.

Whenever another kid had a turn and was trying to blow a bubble, he'd swing at the bubble before it was even finished. When it was his turn, he'd grab the wand and jam it up to his face, but he was too impatient to take aim. I held the wand for him, but he reared his head back and jerked foward, spitting out a breath of air in an action unrelated to the location of the wand.

Then I blew "a million" bubbles for the kids to break, and he spun around, flailing his arms so wildly that he couldn't focus on a bubble or see if he happened to pop one. It wasn't long before his friends lost interest in this unrewarding game and ran off, leaving him behind.

When he started blubbering, I thought I'd quiet him down with some personal attention. I stood up to blow a big bubble that was out of his reach. He was excited, but I waited a few beats before I released it and let it fall into his swing. He got it.

"Good one, you got it," I said calmly, and then blew another big one. Again I waited, and again I let it drift down within his reach. He swung at it, but too wildly, and missed; it popped on the ground. Without saying anything, I slowly blew another. When I let it float down to him, he poked at it and popped it.

As I started to blow the next one, I realized that he was waiting. He knew what was coming; he knew that it was for him, and he knew that he could do it. I gradually allowed the waiting periods to get longer. He started breathing more normally and easily reached for and broke each bubble that came his way.

When I stooped to give him a turn at blowing, he grabbed at the wand. I held it back and told him that I would hold it and he could blow. He squawked an objection, but when I demonstrated a blow, he quickly quieted down and swung at the bubble, bursting it.

"You're good at bubbles, huh?" He looked at me, maybe for the first time. I took my time dipping the wand into the jar and held it out, saying, "OK, your turn, you blow."

This time he didn't grab—he blew a fast blast of air out. It wasn't aimed at the wand, but I was able to move the wand into his airstream. A quick flurry of bubbles emerged, delighting us both. He swung at them, too excited to get any, but I told him, "Hey, you did it! You blew bubbles, you're good at this." He was vibrating again, excited by his success and my praise.

When I told him that it was my turn again, his face flashed with a look of bewilderment, but when I stood up and blew a big bubble, he was back on familiar ground, and when it reached him he swung and popped it. "Good."

When I stroked his head during his turn, he didn't pull away. When I took my time building a more complex form, he waited, patiently. Slowly, he learned to aim his blow. Back and forth, slowly, we learned to take turns.

*A Magic Nation*

# Mustache

In Central Park, there is a paved walkway lined on either side with benches and statues of literary figures. This is the main highway for folks walking from the zoo to the lake. I discovered one day that lurking in that forest of benches was a highwayman with designs on the coins in my pocket.

He appeared suddenly from nowhere, rose up onto a bench, extended his arms, and called out to the passing strangers promises of questions without answers, answers to those questions, reasons to laugh, and laughter without reason. His sudden leap out of the background into the lives of passing strangers has a remarkable hold on my memory.

He was a magician dressed in a brown leather outfit that might have reminded you vaguely of Woodstock, and he wore a Robin Hood cap made from the same brown leather. It was a well-crafted hat that would have stolen the show if not for his mustache: tightly waxed, and ten inches long on each side if it had stuck straight out in both directions. It didn't stick straight out, though; it headed southeast and southwest from his face before spiraling up and encircling his cheekbones. He wore it on him, he carried it, and you realized that he had always had it. This man playing the part of an eccentric was in fact a man with a mustache who dresses up and goes out into the streets to stop people in the middle of their lives to laugh at him while he shows them card tricks. There was something going on here that was not quite the same as acting.

His attempt at an olde English dialect was made ludicrous by his unmistakable New York accent. After his audience groaned at a particularly bad pun, he invited us to at least applaud one side of his mustache (saving the other side for when he might need it later). We did applaud, and we were as grateful for the opportunity as we were delighted to find that he too had noticed this remarkable appendage that held our eye even while his hands labored to fool us.

He made no secret of the fact that he was there to take our money if he could. He intimated that he would stoop to any depth of chicanery or humor to secure some payment from us. What we mostly paid was our attention. I suppose that in the end I did give him some coins, but if so, it is money I can't remember, given to a man I can't quite forget.

# Busking In Berkeley

*Well, the wind isn't real bad for Berkeley. Some gusts, and a background buzz, but the Student Union building is blocking the bulk of it. The lighting isn't perfect either–I'll be in the shadow of the building–but the smoke bubbles will glow and attract attention.*

Stacey, a 15-year-old, street-smart juggler with torches and a top hat, did a snappy show, gathered a big crowd, collected some coin, and is now hanging around to catch my show. We've been trading this spot since lunchtime, and he'll probably take one more turn before we both head over the bridge back to the city.

Ten minutes to three, too early to start. High tide is due in at the hour and the half-hour, when classes change and the students pour down through Strather Gate, across Sproul Plaza, and past me out onto Telegraph Avenue.

It's like the movement of a school of bright fish: upstream, anchored to their literature tables, are politicos and Moonies offering advice and arguments. No big gatherings there; just the few who can be lured in with a line. Below, where the stream widens, are the commercial fishermen, preachers, and other performers, all of us casting our nets to gather large crowds.

Or maybe I'm more like the surfers I watched one day from a pier. They bobbed up and down, lying on their bellies on the sea waiting for a wave. I was right alongside them, but up above. I could even listen to their conversations, but from my lofty position on the pier I could see better than they could how the ocean was acting. I could see the ripples coming, and I tried to guess which would become waves worth riding. Then suddenly one of the surfers started paddling with his hands; he thought a big one was on its way in. I looked back but knew he was wrong–there was nothing coming. Then a second surfer and a third and a fourth started paddling. I looked again, but they were wrong–I could see better than they could, and the water heading in was smooth. Then the sea beneath them welled up and a sweet wave rode three of them along toward the beach while the late starter was left behind with me to just bob up and back down again. They had felt something that I couldn't see.

At five minutes to three I'm spreading out my raggedy puppets along the steps to show the other performers that this stage is taken. Up the way there's a guy with a guitar, and Holy Hubert is already starting to preach, but there are no Krishna chanters or bagpipers in sight, so at least I'll be heard.

At 3:00, it's time to get something started. The flow hasn't reached here yet, but if I can get three people to stop, they'll create enough of an obstruction to the flow that it will look as if a crowd is gathering, and this will attract other folks who will come over to see what the crowd is watching.

I blow a smoke bubble and send it out. It floats a bit but mostly falls; good, at least there's not a steady wind. I make a

*A Magic Nation*

bigger one, but it catches a stray gust and swirls out over the heads of the passersby. Still no one looking, but now the juggler says "Wow!" and a few heads turn. They follow his gaze up to see what might be a solid grey ball floating on the air, indifferent to the laws of gravity. Here comes a bright shiny young couple: she's giggling and talking loudly, and if they stop, something might start. She sees the bubble in her periphery, turns, and says "Wha…" but just then it pops in a silent explosion of smoke. She says "Whoa! did you…?" He turns, but there's nothing. They keep walking while she tries to explain.

Others saw it and there are some laughs, but only a few heads turn to look for the source. I blow another smoke bubble, and this time I'm able to bounce it from one elbow and then the other before this one too catches a breeze out to the center of Sproul Plaza, where it lights up in the sunshine, then dives down to burst on the shoulder of a man with his back turned. The tide has turned, the plaza is crowded, and lots of folks saw that.

I blow another smoke bubble and let it hang from the wand. Suddenly, I have a lot of attention. They are not yet an audience, but they are a crowd. I touch the top of the wand and a stream of smoke shoots up in a straight column as the bubble quickly deflates. One sound comes from the crowd: they all let out their breath at the same time. Now if I talk to enough people at once, they'll be an audience.

"Howdy folks, my name is Tom Noddy and what I do is called Bubble Magic; I blow bubbles inside of bubbles, smoke bubbles, clear bubbles, clear bubbles inside of smoke bubbles, smoke bubbles inside of clear bubbles, inside-out bubbles, yin yang bubbles, caterpillar bubbles, love bubbles, and a bubble cube…"

At the sound of a voice, the audience quickly triples in size. I feel the wave but I've still got to paddle if I hope to ride it.

"…and the yin yang bubble is a double bubble: a smoke bubble and a clear bubble with a smoke bubble in the clear bubble and a clear bubble in the smoke bubble. It's my most difficult trick–to say."

The crowd laughs with one voice. Now they are my audience and I'm at the crest of a wave, hoping to ride this liquid flow.

# Rick's Story

My friend Rick took a college class in physics from a teacher who wanted to explain some of the basic laws. One fact she wanted to demonstrate is that the shortest distance between two points is a straight line. Because she is a good teacher, she tried to find a way to show the students in that coastal California town how this information might be useful.

She asked them to imagine that they were lifeguards seated at their stations at the beach and that they saw a swimmer in trouble. To get to the drowning person, should they run in a zigzag pattern? A loop? A straight line? What's the fastest way? Nearly everyone gave her the answer she was looking for: run straight toward the swimmer. That's the shortest distance between the lifeguard and the swimmer.

Rick, a surfer who spends a lot of time at the beach, had a different and better answer: he would run straight ahead to the wet sand, where he would have better footing, and then across that firmer sand until he was opposite the swimmer.

Rick didn't violate the laws of physics, but by adding his own experience, he was able to effectively transfer the theoretical knowledge he learned in school to the real world, where it might actually help.

# Obsession

I understand that other people aren't as obsessed with soap bubbles as I am, but I can't say that I understand why.

Bubbles are bright little sprites that tease as they flit in and out of your life; they know how to have fun with a gust of wind or a beam of light. Their forces are balanced, their angles are equal; they're fragile and flexible, tension and compression, yin and yang, positive and negative, Laurel and Hardy. A bubble is an ultra-high-frequency geodesic event; it's a breath encased in little more than a mist. Bubbles are cheap to buy, easy to make, and you're allowed to break them; they please your parents and babysit your kids.

After 17 years of playing with bubbles almost every day, I see them everywhere, not just as sea foam and as air pockets in bread, but as atoms and their electromagnetic fields, as the earth and the atmosphere around it, the moon and its gravitational aura, the stars and their spheres of influence, the political and religious boundaries where ideas meet, the romantic boundaries where souls meet.

*Tom Noddy's Bubble Magic*

# BUBBLIOGRAPHY

Frederick J. Almgren, Jr., and Jean E. Taylor, "The Geometry of Soap Films and Soap Bubbles" *(Scientific American* Magazine, July, 1976).

This article provided a new mathematical model for understanding the basic laws that govern the geometry of soap films. In so doing, the authors have solved one of the longest-standing problems of mathematics. Anyone hoping to advance our understanding of this subject should first read this article.

C.V. Boys, *Soap-Bubbles, Their Colours and Forces Which Mould Them* (New York: Dover, 1911, 1959).

Boys was a professor at Oxford who gave a very popular series of lectures on the science of soap bubbles to groups of junior high school-aged students in the 1890s. His words are still in print and widely available. For anyone with a limited knowledge of mathematics but a further interest in the science of soap bubbles, this is a comprehensive and readable book on the subject.

**Paul G. Hewitt, *Conceptual Physics, 5th ed.*** (Boston: Little, Brown & Co., 1985).

Mr. Hewitt is able to explain some very complicated concepts while maintaining a healthy sense of humor. If this had been my textbook while I was in school, it might not have taken years of playing with bubbles to stir my interest in physics.

**Stefan Hildebrandt and Anthony Tromba, *Mathematics and Optimal Form*** (New York: Scientific American Books, 1985).

Written by two top mathematicians, this book asks why nature produces certain forms and why it prefers them to other conceivable forms. Starting with the history of mathematics as it applies to this question and proceeding to very modern applications, this will be especially interesting to students of mathematics. The photos and other illustrations are especially fascinating.

**Cyril Isenberg, *The Science of Soap Films and Soap Bubbles*** (Avon, England: Tieto Ltd., 1978).

This is the most comprehensive work on soap bubbles that I have encountered. Isenberg has dedicated his book to C.V. Boys, but he has written for the student who is not afraid of mathematics.

**J.A.F. Plateau, *Statique Expérimentale et Théorique des Liquides*** (Paris: Gauthier-Villars, 1873).

Plateau was a blind Belgian physicist whose years of careful "observations" of soap bubbles laid the foundation of all that is now known about the science of soap bubbles. Basic questions posed by Plateau (called the Plateau problems) are still unanswered by mathematicians today.

**Peter S. Stevens, *Patterns in Nature*** (Boston: Little, Brown & Co., 1974).

Stevens has written a very readable book that brings the seemingly random patterns in nature within the grasp of the general reader.

**D'Arcy Thompson, *On Growth and Form, 2nd ed.*** (Cambridge: Cambridge University Press, 1952).

By observing the forms preferred by nature, from the branching of trees and rivers to the structures of soap bubbles, Thompson continues to inspire students of nature to look closely.

**Bernie Zubrowski, *Bubbles*** (Boston: Little, Brown & Co., 1979).

Written for children, this book from the designer of science exhibits for Boston's Children's Museum is a fun introduction to the idea of learning through the use of playful experiments.